Did We
Meet On
Grub Street?

Did We Meet On Grub Street?

a publishing miscellany

Emma Tennant
Hilary Bailey
& David Elliott

QUARTET

First published in 2014 by Quartet Books Limited
A member of the Namara Group
27 Goodge Street, London W1T 2LD
Copyright © Emma Tennant, Hilary Bailey and
David Elliott 2014
The right of Emma Tennant, Hilary Bailey and
David Elliott to be identified
as the authors of this work has been asserted
by them in accordance with the
Copyright, Designs and Patents Act, 1988
A catalogue record for this book
is available from the British Library
ISBN 978 0 7043 7298 6
Typeset by Josh Bryson
Printed and bound in Great Britain by
T J International Ltd, Padstow, Cornwall

*'To live is to war with trolls in heart and soul. To write is to sit
in judgement on oneself.'*

Henrik Ibsen

INTRODUCTION
David Elliott

Now it's a rounded, glass-topped, airport terminal-type building (which you can see from before Oxford Circus if you are looking west along Oxford Street) which looms out like the bigger-than-everyone-else's hats of HRH the Duchess of Cornwall at royal occasions. The British Steel brutal tower block which was there when I was there could never be seen from that far away. For a time, when the world's financial system collapsed the last time round, it was a hole in the ground, suitable for dinosaurs-that-moved exhibitions as a Christmas treat to rival the Santa in Selfridge's department store almost opposite, across the road. Once, half a century ago, when Mr Holly travelled in early December in a horse and carriage along Oxford Street ringing a bell, with Santa sitting by him, to be welcomed outside the department store by children singing carols, I worked in Claude Gill Books, a bookshop squeezed between the fashion stores, in the shadow of the now demolished tower.

It's a demolished time now, I suppose: when booksellers were once taught to sell books. Rather than now, as they stand behind computer terminals tapping on their keyboards like airline ticket clerks searching for seat reservations, or stick notes of illiterate love underneath pop-star memoirs or current potboilers to entice our interest in 'staff pick' sections which make their shops look like infant school activity corners.

Maybe book buyers have been demolished, or at least the book buyers I knew. Listen to this. Before I was first allowed to deal alone with customers on the actual shop floor, I had to stand beside a more experienced bookseller as their customer was paying (or having their account charged against) next to a large silver cash till with ten drawers that opened individually, depending on which bookseller was 'making the sale'. (This *was* 1971 and even fuddy-duddy bookshop workers knew management-speak in those Harold Wilson 'white heat of technology' times. We all had training sessions then, utilising the government grants that materialised during the mighty decimalisation campaign when guineas – hardback novels were nearly always priced in guineas – became new pence.) The till was operated by having its keys pressed down, rather like a typewriter, with a handle on the side to be cranked whenever the respective drawer was to be opened, but it was fuelled by electricity. It took at least six people to carry it and its ornate side pieces could sometimes fall off, risking damaging a customer's toe or two.

Back to the transaction, though, where at this point I took the book or books from my more senior colleague and after asking a question of the customer would place the purchase on a side table next to the large silver till and create a brown paper parcel, or place in a white paper bag, the book or books, dependent on the customer's answer. And the question – listen – was whether the customer wished to have the dust-wrapper removed or left on the book? Wrapper-removed books were folded into brown paper parcels and wrapper-retained were placed in paper bags, though customers could, if required, have parcels made for dust-wrapped books if bought in quantity.

Everyone was asked the same question, everyone except those who bought paperbacks. Customers who bought paperbacks weren't spoken to very much at all. Paperbacks were stuffed higgledy-piggledy into warehouse shelves right at the back of the ground floor, categorised by the publishing imprint alone. If you didn't know that Nevil Shute was published by Pan Books (who now remembers Nevil Shute? Who now remembers Pan Books?) you were stuffed just as badly as the books were.

That time is this book's starting point, though we'll cast a look back further at where we all came from: the book trade, forty odd years ago, just before the nouveau spivs got power.

And maybe one more anecdote might give you a flavour of then…

William Collins was still an independent publisher, with printing presses and offices in Glasgow, where its bibles, dictionaries, atlases and phrase books were managed, but its general publishing activity and more important executives worked from rather grand offices just of St James's in Mayfair, where all the hedge funds now inhabit – proper, grown-up spivs at least. The twice-yearly sales conferences were held in Glasgow and here's the rub: the editorial staff travelled up to Glasgow Central in first-class carriages; the sales and publicity people travelled in second. Which I suppose creates a good enough definition of a book trade spiv that I know of – the sales person in second class who wants to travel first. In this trade, resentment always motivates wealth, if played correctly.

Emma Tennant and Hilary Bailey had already been published by the time I started selling books properly, though I had been a bookseller of sorts, working for six years previously in the mail order and library supply department at Claude Gill. Emma's first novel, *The Colour of Rain*, was published under a pseudonym in 1963 but I got to know her name more when she started and edited the literary magazine, *Bananas*, in 1975. Hilary's first novel, *The Black Corridor*, was co-authored with her then husband, Michael Moorcock, and published in 1969. Both of them have written well over forty books, even two together, since then. And I managed a few including an account of my book trade career, of which more later.

Two other book trade craftsmen will contribute material to this miscellany: Naim Attallah and Ian Norrie. Naim become

3

my boss when he persuaded me to join Quartet Books thirty-seven years ago and Ian, a fiercely independent and successful Hampstead bookseller for many years, let me publish his last two contributions to his lifetime's devotion to writing the history of the British book trade. Ian would not agree totally with everything I say and, alas, he's no longer around to ask, but his knowledge was profound and much of what he wrote is still pertinent, so it's right to include him.

> *...he made half a success; that is to say, the publishers brought out a second edition of the book.*
> **George Gissing, *New Grub Street***

So what's this book about? What's it for? Well, hopefully, first and foremost it will be enjoyed. Around the time I started selling books on Oxford Street and Santa rode into Selfridge's, Hutchinson would issue yet another *Saturday Book*, edited by John Hadfield. An annual, it came in its own box (a nuisance for booksellers as browsers seemed incapable of putting lids back on boxes without damaging their corners) with a potpourri of essays, stories and illustrations celebrating some cultural theme or other. Its production standards were way beyond the call of duty with printed art paper, beautifully designed endpapers, proper sewn headbands and a cloth binding. Illustrated colour sections were interspersed with profuse black and white photographic sections and woodcarvings, or specially commissioned drawings complemented many of the essays and stories. Its appearance was more important than its contents, though a troll through ancient second-hand copies for sale for peanuts on Abe Books' website (though most seem minus box or jackets and are mighty foxed) reveal a list of contributors who included most of the great English (mostly male) writers of the last century, from H. E. Bates to Evelyn Waugh. It died in 1975, killed off by Monty Python, *The Guinness Book of Records* and BBC tie-in editions of multi-part culture shows by Kenneth Clark, Jacob Bronowski, et al. The Christmas gift market always moves on…but the concept of a miscellany, *A Saturday Book* with a little of this and that, about the last half-century in the book trade seems appropriate as publishers become 'content providers', Google fight Amazon for ebook ascendancy, libraries dwindle, bookshops close and more children leave our schools illiterate than at any time since government records began.

Will Grub Street even be open for business ten or twenty years from now?

He had no difficulty in deciding how to use this money. His mother's desire to live in London had in him the force of an inherited motive; as soon as possible he released himself from his uncongenial occupations, converted into money all the possessions of which he had not immediate need, and betook himself to the metropolis. To become a literary man, of course.

His capital lasted him nearly four years, for, notwithstanding his age, he lived with painful economy. The strangest life, of almost absolute loneliness. From a certain point of Tottenham Court Road there is visible a certain garret window in a certain street which runs parallel with that thoroughfare; for the greater part of these four years the garret in question was Reardon's home. He paid only three-and-sixpence a week for the privilege of living there; his food cost him about a shilling a day; on clothing and other unavoidable expenses he laid out some five pounds yearly. Then he bought books – volumes which cost anything between twopence and two shillings; further than that he durst not go. A strange time, I assure you.

When he had completed his twenty-first year, he desired to procure a reader's ticket for the British Museum. Now this was not such a simple matter as you may suppose; it was necessary to obtain the signature of some respectable householder, and Reardon was acquainted with no such person. His landlady was a decent woman enough, and a payer of rates and taxes, but it would look odd, to say the least of it, to present oneself in Great Russell Street armed with this person's recommendation. There was nothing for it but to take a bold step, to force himself upon the attention of a stranger – the thing from which his pride had always shrunk.

He wrote to a well-known novelist – a man with whose works he had some sympathy. 'I am trying to prepare myself for a literary career. I wish to study in the Reading Room of the British Museum, but have no

*acquaintance to whom I can refer in the ordinary way.
Will you help me – I mean, in this particular only?'
That was the substance of his letter. For reply came an
invitation to a house in the West End. With fear and
trembling Reardon answered the summons.*

*He was so shabbily attired; he was so diffident from
the habit of living quite alone; he was horribly afraid lest
it should be supposed that he looked for other assistance
than he had requested. Well, the novelist was a rotund
and jovial man; his dwelling and his person smelt of
money; he was so happy himself that he could afford to
be kind to others.*

*'Have you published anything?' he enquired, for the
young man's letter had left this uncertain.*

*'Nothing. I have tried the magazines, but as yet
without success.'*

'But what do you write?'

'Chiefly essays on literary subjects.'

*'I can understand that you would find a difficulty in
disposing of them. That kind of thing is supplied either
by men of established reputation, or by anonymous
writers who have a regular engagement on papers and
magazines. Give me an example of your topics.'*

'I have written something lately about Tibullus.'

*'Oh, dear! Oh, dear! – Forgive me, Mr Reardon; my
feelings were too much for me; those names have been my
horror ever since I was a schoolboy. Far be it from me to
discourage you, if your line is to be solid literary criticism;
I will only mention, as a matter of fact, that such work
is indifferently paid and in very small demand. It hasn't
occurred to you to try your hand at fiction?'*

*In uttering the word he beamed; to him it meant a
thousand or so a year.*

'I am afraid I have no talent for that.'

*The novelist could do no more than grant his genial
signature for the specified purpose, and add good wishes
in abundance.*

Reardon went home with his brain in a whirl. He had had his first glimpse of what was meant by literary success. That luxurious study, with its shelves of handsomely bound books, its beautiful pictures, its warm, fragrant air – great heavens! What might not a man do who sat at his ease amid such surroundings!
George Gissing, ***New Grub Street***

Let's begin with Hilary's guide to getting published...

DOS AND DONT'S FOR FUTURE WRITERS
Hilary Bailey

Well, to begin with – DON'T think anyone can tell you how to write a book. It's like so many things, trying to assemble flat-pack furniture, for example, the instructions are all very well, actually turning them into a chest of drawers is a very different thing.

But – DO – enjoy yourself. Admit it: unless you're writing under contract to pay the bills and feed the family, you're writing a book because you want to. So enjoy it or stop. There's no need to split yourself into two people – the stern teacher asking where the homework is and the pupil with nothing in the backpack. That way madness lies.

Once you stop beating yourself up you may be forced to admit you're writing in order to be published, have your name on the spine, become rich and famous, attract beautiful women and at last gain respect from your family. The first three (if you're male) are attainable, just about. There are plenty of women who will go out with an ugly, famous, rich writer. You can marry one – then another – then another.

For women the prospects are dimmer. Men don't particularly like women who write. This was well summed up by Lord Byron when his ex-mistress, Lady Caroline Lamb, depicted him unflatteringly in her novel *Glenarvon*. 'Never mind the woman who kisses and tells,' wrote the bard. 'Beware of the one who fucks and writes.' As for gaining the respect of your family – forget it. They think you will give away their secrets. You can win the Nobel

Prize for Literature but they'll still feel annoyed about that portrait of cousin Charlie in your novel (even if it wasn't) and fear you'll do worse in your next – hint that your dad was a London cabbie or your mum always drunk or Uncle Robert destroyed Grandad's will. Far from respecting you, they'll probably never forgive you.

In the meanwhile, enjoy yourself. The Goncourt brothers' *Journal* tell of a party where the novelist Gustave Flaubert, borrowing a tail coat from the critic, Theophile Gautier, and, messing up his own hair, got up after dinner and performed an act called 'The Idiot's Dance'. Not to be outdone, Gautier joined in and performed 'The Creditor's Dance'. If two shining geniuses in an age of geniuses were prepared to put their hats on backwards and perform a Parisian version of the Egyptian Sand Dance, then why are you sitting in the pub complaining about your writers' block?

DO – remember most books are like Caesar's Gaul, divided into three parts. The first part establishes, the second part develops, the third resolves. The second part is the hardest. In the nineteenth century, when books were published in three volumes, the novelist George Eliot would always groan over what she called 'the middle volume'.

DO – bear in mind that most fiction is written for two people: the writer and the reader. Getting the balance right is the challenge. Part of it is that what you, the author, are writing about must appeal to others. The other part of it is that some writers can describe a wet Wednesday in Widnes and the reader won't be able to stop reading. Others can be telling you about the hunt for Bin Laden in the Torah Borah Mountains and the reader won't care; as the Hollywood director said in the 1930s, when the city was full of émigré film makers, 'To be Hungarian is not enough. You must also have talent.' And that is another subject.

DON'T – look for 'material'. It doesn't exist.

DON'T – bother to write if you're tired, bored, or hungover. You will carry your readers with you, but only into a world of feeling tired, bored, headachy and queasy.

DO – decide if your novel is a crime novel, or a science-fiction novel or an historical novel, because books are a commodity like breakfast cereals; they have their own fans, their own units in publishing companies, and their own dedicated, labelled shelf space in bookshops and you, the author, need to declare where your book fits in.

If you are in the category of the oddly named 'literary fiction' then it gets more complicated. It was probably only at the beginning of the twentieth century that the distinction between 'art' and 'craft' in fiction was properly defined. Up to that point writers wrote what other writers wrote – sensational novels, adventure tales, tales of the supernatural – only some did it much better than others. But later it became clear that Henry James was an artist, Arthur Conan Doyle a craftsman – one wanted the others' large sales, the big-selling writer wanted the other's reputation. Some things never change.

Up to that point writers such as Shakespeare, writing to a deadline, conscious of the fact that half the audience was standing up, coughing, eating nuts, urinating into buckets hung just below the stage and giving each other fatal diseases, had to deal in an unselfconscious way with the problem of writing what they wanted to write and what could keep the groundlings happy – just another problem. The 'intelligent play' and the 'literary novel' came later. Still, most 'literary novels' are now historical novels. Unless they are thrillers.

In the meanwhile, the novelist would do well to find a category and put his or her novel in it, even if it doesn't fit very well. It reassures agents, editors, and booksellers.

DON'T – upset the susceptibilities of the middle classes. They are the people who buy books. And most agents and editors are middle class.

The middle classes are, so to speak, the colonial power. They are the norm. The onlookers. Others are objects of interest, sympathy, and so forth but they are the Other. So it's unwise to suggest that except in rare instances the middle classes can be greedy, cruel to their children, nasty to work colleagues, fanatical about religion or politics, alcoholic, drug-addicted or broke (adultery is OK).

Fine if you come from one of the observed sections – a housing estate, a foreign background – your ethnic or working-class credentials entitle you to write a kind of travelogue fiction from Glasgow, Brixton, or Southall. Careful, though. We must remember Israel Zangwill, born and bred in the overcrowded, immigrant East End in the early part of the twentieth century, began with sympathetic chronicles of the lives of poor Jewish immigrants and ended up caricaturing them for an audience that was not them.

The middle classes are the subject; immigrants, the working class, people on housing estates, footballers' wives, rap artists, peers, practically everyone else, are the objects. Thoreau wrote, 'Most men lead lives of quiet desperation and go to the grave with the song still in them.' Probably true, but a lot of people prefer it that way. Don't startle the bourgeoisie. Consolation, not challenge, is required.

DO – keep an eye on the time. Not yours, the book's. Novels in particular are about time.

The French Connection
As Boileau wrote, '*Qu'en un lieu, qu'en un jour, un seul fait accompli, Tienne just a la fin le theatre rempli.*' The three unities for the theatre – one sequence of events taking place in one place and, on one day, an idea that never took off properly in English drama. But while you can prescribe like this for the theatre, the novel is a ragbag; you can go back and forth in

time and have a cast of thousands. The only limitations are the writer's and the reader's imaginations.

Look at Proust, for example. But: not too much flashback.

It is not a good idea to have more than three dates on any given page, i.e., the time as is, and another, in the form of a flashback. So let us say that Jack, in the here and now, is drinking a cup of tea and remembering what his grandfather told him about landing in Dunkirk in 1940. It is not a good idea if, on the same page, the reader is faced with Jack as a boy falling out of a tree in 1980, unless there is a very good reason for it. If there is not, jump out of the Tardis, slow down and give the readers a break.

It is often useful to head a long retrospective passage or chapter with the date. And place. This saves a lot of time dropping clues to the reader about where and when the action is occurring, and because the clues are only there as clues they are often sections of very battered and familiar scenery – the newspaper-seller bawling something out about assassinations in Sarajevo or shocking murders in Whitechapel – glimpses of the Bois de Boulogne in Spring – St Paul's Cathedral through the fog – the tramp of clogs down a cobbled street at dawn – 'Will there be war, do you think?'

Sometimes there is a need to hold back information when writing, to create mystery, to unveil a situation slowly – many reasons. But pointlessly withholding useful information, perhaps to attract attention, is as annoying in fiction as it can be in life. It doesn't make reading any more interesting, just hard work.

DON'T – tell people you're writing a book (or not many); they may not think better of you, because in Britain, or perhaps just in England, people have no particular respect for writers. In other countries, attitudes may be different but in Britain/England, in spite of producing considerable writers, writing is not considered serious, and may in fact involve a lot of people who hang around the house in their pyjamas all day when they should be going out to work or otherwise engaged in useful tasks.

'Another damned, thick square book! Always, scribble, scribble, scribble! Eh! Mr Gibbon?' said the Duke of Gloucester, the King's brother, when the author presented him with the first volume of his mighty *Decline and Fall of the Roman Empire*. To be fair it's not just writers who are so seen; painters, sculptors, and composers come in for much the same treatment.

This is worse if you are a man. Writing books is not considered a manly occupation and is only justified by huge success and ostentatious heterosexuality.

Apart from that, once you've mentioned your project those you've told will ask about your progress. If you tell them, they'll be bored. If you don't, they'll assume you're failing.

Having finished your book you may be tempted to tell others about your contacts with agents and publishers and what they said, or didn't say about the book. DON'T.

There are some subjects which on the whole you should not say too much about – the route from A to B, for example – building repairs to your home – the relationships of your child with other children in his class – soap operas on TV – trainspotting – small lawsuits you are involved in – laundry work – train delays – well, the list of subjects others may not care to hear about is tedious in itself.

Regrettably, your dealings with publishers, agents, readers, etc. come into this category. They sometimes veer into self-pity, rage, and incipient paranoia.

Remember – you have an illness. People are kind and sympathetic but they don't want every detail of your symptoms, your medical appointments, your medication, and the fruits of your internet researches into your disease, still less do they want to hear that the doctors and nurses are all against you, as is the whole medical establishment. They ought to want to, but they don't. They just do not.

There are probably only three statements you can safely make about writing a book. 'I'm writing a book.' 'I've finished my book.' 'I've sold my book – crack out the champagne.' This is sad, but true.

On the same subject – DON'T – take comments made by agents, readers, publishers, publishers' readers, too deeply to heart. Those who write these comments are not academics, they have not made a deep, accurate, almost forensic investigation of your work. They are, as we are told, busy people who read a great many manuscripts (no one ever asks why, if they're too busy, they don't take on more staff). Their comments are a rough impression of what they think, not so much an Ordnance Survey as something scrawled on the back of an envelope in a rain storm. Although sometimes the criticisms can be spot on, others are unclear and generalised – to attempt to decode them and assume they could or should be translated precisely into action is probably a mistake. You may wreck your book.

Feedback

It's baffling that this is called 'feedback' which is where you speak or sing into a mike and it screeches back at you.

DO – consider that there may be good ideas, bad ideas and ideas. 'Where do you get your ideas from?' people ask; or as Shakespeare wrote:

> *Tell me where is Fancy bred,*
> *In the heart or in the head?*
> *How begot, how nourished?*

For practical purposes there are three kinds of ideas: good ideas, bad ideas, and Capital I ideas – political, social, philosophical, religious, scientific and ethical.

Serious Ideas

Capital I ideas are hard. The novel as a means of exposing social ills has a long tradition. The criticisms come mostly from the radical side (Ayn Rand excepted). Dickens exposed horrible conditions in schools in *Nicholas Nickleby*, Charlote Brontë the same in *Jane Eyre* (though that was personal as she and her sisters had been subjected to one). Dickens, again, wrote of the hardships of industrial cities in *Hard Times* in the 1850s and the novelist, Mrs Gaskell, also in the 1850s, in *North and South*. Mrs Gaskell, wife of a Manchester minister at the time, certainly knew all about it, though both authors were queasy about organised labour and particularly about strikes; for them, a supporter of unions and strikes was an agitator, little better than an anarchist. From there, via Zola's *Germinal* to Upton Sinclair's novel about conditions in the Chicago stockyards of 1906, and Steinbeck's *The Grapes of Wrath*, about dustbowl America during the Depression, social ideas are not a problem – but it's hard to write about philosophy in a novel. Some readers of Jean-Paul Sartre's sequence of novels might agree. Some readers of Voltaire's *Candide* would argue the other way.

Religion is tricky, too, when you think of Milton's too-attractive Satan and the perfunctory-seeming injection of Christianity in Graham Greene's novels.

It doesn't help that in fiction virtue is so often uninteresting. It is hard to think of an exception to this rule. When Natasha Rostov is a giddy, lively but sometimes misguided girl in *War and Peace*, we love her; seldom has a young woman been so well-seen, by an author of either sex. Once she is married Tolstoy loses all his affection for her, he promotes her as an ideal wife and she loses any character or liveliness she once possessed. As far as the rest of us are concerned, Natasha might as well be dead.

On the whole, Big Ideas are great but have to be handled with care. Aside from the fact that they date, as a new Idea supersedes the old, the temptation of the author may be to lecture and inform, which readers of the respectable middle classes take on gallantly, but often without enjoying themselves much.

Nevertheless, long may authors continue to inform, to expose, and to discuss.

Mundane Ideas

It's said that there are only sixteen plots in the world – or it may be sixty-six – but no one seems to know what they are. Similarly all books carry a message, however simple; that women need husbands, men need to right wrongs; that war is hell; that we seek and find; that individuals and families set out on a journey which can end well or badly.

Finding the Idea

It is worrying to see someone looking for an idea for a book, a story or a poem, like watching someone with a toothache. You can't help; only they can do something about it but, can they, will they? Meanwhile they scan the landscape wild-eyed, as if a knight were going to come riding over the hill at a gallop with a pennant streaming behind him bearing the message: 'This is the idea for your next book.' They scan the faces of those they meet in an unnerving way, as if the faces bore a clue. They create little mouses' nests of abandoned bits of paper. A remark such as: 'Relax. It'll come to you,' is about as useful as: 'Try not to think about the pain.'

The history of science is full of Eureka moments – Newton and the apple, George Stevenson and the boiling kettle. Literary history too has its recorded moments. Remember Mr Rochester's final blindness, which evened the balance of power between Jane Eyre and Rochester. Mary Shelley began *Frankenstein*, famously, in Switzerland, when unusually bad weather had kept one of the most famous holidays-with-another-couple in history confined to the house. Byron challenged those present – Shelley, Mary, Mary's half-sister Claire who was Byron's lover and his doctor, who was with the party – to write a supernatural tale. Mary dreamed that night, 'I saw a pale student of unhallowed arts kneeling beside the thing he had put together.' The student was of course Frankenstein, the thing, his monster.

Good Ideas and Bad Ideas

Ideas got on holiday or visits to strange places should be treated with caution.

Many would have preferred Flaubert to have written *Madame Bovary: The Sequel* instead of *Salammbo*, his less widely-read novel of third-century BC Carthage. The same could be said of George Eliot's *Romola* (fifteenth-century Florence). The trouble is that the brain is stimulated by a trip; even the exercise involved – climbing the steps to the cathedral, walking up hills for a picnic – may have provided stimulation and the author may be tricked into thinking this is a Good Idea as opposed to any old idea.

Other ideas to beware of are – paragraphs in newspapers – stories strangers tell you in the pub or on trains – TV programmes. The trouble is: any of these may actually be good ideas, the one you've been waiting for. There are no recipes.

The Muses

The Greeks personified the creative spirit. The muses were its goddesses and one of the nine – memory, comedy, lyric, song, tragedy, dance, erotic poetry, sacred song and astronomy – had to be on your side when you wrote, danced, sang. And it didn't work if the Muse was absent. We don't believe this now, but the odd thing is that we might as well, because we don't ever know quite why sometimes imagination comes readily, and sometimes not.

These days we don't believe in the Muses although men used to have muses, not statues in flowing drapery, but live women who had to look after Bohemian households and put up with the vagaries of the artistic temperament. That kind of muse has gone somewhat out of date these days, perhaps as a result of better job opportunities for women. What happens sometimes when a poet requires a Muse and his wife is not a Muse but another poet is shown in the lives, and deaths, of Ted Hughes and Sylvia Plath.

DO – stop in time. Readers are quite intelligent. It is easy to end a paragraph with a sentence encapsulating what that paragraph showed but it won't be necessary. Readers would prefer to see something happen than be told about it.

DON'T – give your spouse, children, friends, and relations a hard time just because you're writing a book. Especially children, who will grow up and write other books saying what a monster you were, detailing tantrums and the flinging of teapots and chairs. It's not much good anyway, having someone in the house who's only half there, the other half being in Chapter 9 – that thousand-yard stare into the baby's eyes is very poor child-rearing and should be banned by social services – but you can at least try to control the shouting, reproaches, self-pity, and chucking stuff about.

DON'T – think you have to keep going when you are too tired. Some jobs can be done when you're dropping, like digging, scrubbing, and hauling heavy burdens. Some have to be done when you're dropping, like feeding babies. But you don't do hard crosswords or operate delicate machinery when you're tired, or not successfully, and writing is much the same.

Writing involves making constant, often complex choices, all the time. Invent – accept – discard. Invent – accept – discard. You may not be conscious of making these choices, but you are. So get some sleep.

DO – find a place to write. This will obviously depend on your personal circumstances but the traditional places to write, cafes, attics, and spare rooms, are not so good in these days of Starbucks and the almost total absence of attics and spare rooms in our crowded houses.

Virginia Woolf said in 1929 that 'a woman must have money and a room of her own if she is to write fiction'. Now we wonder why she specified 'a woman'. But she was probably talking about a world where girls were expected to live at home until marriage and, whether married or single, be expected to be busy, visible, and available at all times, even in households where there were servants doing the actual housekeeping. Trollope's heroines are always up at the crack of dawn to breakfast with their menfolk before journeys, and there at tea-time to pour the tea, even though presumably there were servants to do the basic provisioning. So that room of one's own is perhaps to do with the freedom to be absent and uninterruptable, the reality being that women are more interruptable than men.

Thus it is that women traditionally write on the kitchen table and men in the garden shed until they are successful and prosperous; that is, when obviously things change. The Brontë sisters, as Charlotte Brontë's friend, the novelist Mrs Gaskell, tells us in her biography of her, wrote in the parlour, but only after 9pm when they allowed themselves to put down their sewing. Jane Austen wrote in the drawing room, hiding her work under a blotter when visitors were announced.

Joseph Conrad wrote in a garden shed up a flight of steps which his arthritic wife had to drag herself up to deliver his meals. He lived like this for two years as he wrote *Nostromo*, but apparently regretted it in later life. Proust had his room lined with cork in order to exclude any outside noise.

The beauty of writing books is that it is relatively inexpensive and, unlike the work of painters, for example, the practitioner does not need much space. These days, since few people write by hand or use typewriters, it demands a power point for a computer. But there's usually a power point in a kitchen and cables can be run into garden sheds. The real snag is that while some people can concentrate on what they're doing while the house is on fire, others need peace and quiet.

DON'T – moralise overtly. And letting your main character pontificate is only disguised morality, which fools no one. As the Hollywood director said, 'When you want to show a character in a film is bad, have him come in in the first five minutes and kick a dog.' The same rules apply to making a moral point. Prove it – show us. Show us the oil spill, the slum, the palace, the men and women conspiring one way and another to destroy our happiness and well-being. Albert Camus, a man of strong political and philosophical convictions, said, 'Fiction is a lie through which we tell the truth.' He did not mean by lecturing the readers.

One practical disadvantage to telling the reader what you, or your main character, believes about politics, philosophy, the ecology, and the nature of everything is that it can date your book. What concerns us now may seem trivial tomorrow. For example, all those novels about the threat of Communism will now only stand because of the writing (as with John le Carré). In addition, you can alienate the reader who may not share your views and so will lose sympathy for the book (perhaps you don't care) – the reader might not want any views at all – or might be better informed than you are on the subject of what you're banging on about. Technically, your disquisitions slow down the action of the book, change the mood, affect the structure.

Imagine the court of fiction as a court of law, requiring evidence (through the fiction) and intolerant of hearsay or statements un-backed by facts. So shut up, or the gavel goes down.

DO – get out your library card, Kindle, or borrow a book from a friend who has one. Read, in short.

Even now, when there are many courses teaching you how to write a book and many books telling you how to write a book, it is still a good idea to read one, preferably more than one. Otherwise you're like someone who has been to art school and never seen a painting, or plumbing school and has never seen a pipe. You are like some brilliant alien, on another planet, studying humankind who has never walked, breathed, or been on earth.

There is something to be said for finding a model for the kind of book you want to write, studying and copying it, pretty much. It is a real rope to hang on to when starting out.

But wider reading can help if the model becomes limiting, no longer a support but a constraint. It's not unusual for a writer who has been successful writing about a particular investigator, for example, or a fantasy hero, or any other writer in a sequence of genre novels, to get thoroughly fed up with his or her hero or heroine and/or the limitations of the genre itself. This often shows; the readers are disappointed: X's new Inspector McIndoe novel is not as good as the last. Or Y's latest *Arco, Man of Fire* book doesn't deliver the same thrill. The reason may be that X is sick and tired of Inspector McIndoe and is only carrying on because he has a three-book contract, just for the money or perhaps because of enthusiastic fan letters. At that stage, wider reading can be a breath of fresh air – there is a world outside the crime novel, the fantasy novel, and Inspector McIndoe or Arco aren't in it. Arthur Conan Doyle famously killed off Sherlock Holmes then had to bring him back again. He said this was because his mother had asked him to do so.

You might argue an author would be glad to be stuck with the immensely popular Sherlock but even if you have not been so blessed you might still consider reading a book. There are many strands to the writing of fiction and it is useful to see how many authors do the weaving. Art and craft go hand in hand. Tricks of the trade should not be despised.

Once upon a time when dinosaurs roamed the earth there was a group of writers who knew that somewhere in the world was, or had been, a magic formula for writing fiction. This was called *Lester Dent's Master Plot Finder*. If only, these writers thought, they could lay hands on Lester Dent's masterwork, their problems would be over – but no one knew where it was. Now, thanks to the magic of the internet, it has been discovered and is available to all. Perhaps it was not the Holy Grail it was believed to be before anyone had ever seen it – but here, for your instruction, your delectation and delight, is Lester Dent's Formula. It is by a master pulp-writer. Its recommendations may not apply to a million-word *roman-fleuve*. Readers of distinction may hold their noses but the structural tips are still handy. It's not bad and it's here anyway.

Thisis a formula, a master plot, for any 6000-word pulp
story. It has worked on adventure, detective, western
and war. It tells exactly where to put everything. It
shows definitely just what must happen in each successive 1000
words.

No yarn of mine written to the formula has yet failed to sell.

The business of building stories seems not much different from
the business of building anything else.

Here's how it starts:

1. A DIFFERENT MURDER METHOD FOR VILLAIN
   TO USE
2. A DIFFERENT THING FOR VILLAIN TO BE
   SEEKING
3. A DIFFERENT LOCALE
4. A MENACE WHICH IS TO HANG LIKE A CLOUD
   OVER HERO

One of these DIFFERENT things would be nice, two better,
three swell. It may help if they are fully in mind before tackling
the rest.

A different murder method could be – different. Thinking
of shooting, knifing, hydrocyanic, garrotting, poison needles,
scorpions, a few others, and writing them on paper gets them
where they may suggest something. Scorpions and their poison
bite? Maybe mosquitoes or flies treated with deadly germs?

If the victims are killed by ordinary methods, but found
under strange and identical circumstances each time, it might
serve, the reader of course not knowing until the end, that the
method of murder is ordinary. Scribes who have their villain's
victims found with butterflies, spiders or bats stamped on them
could conceivably be flirting with this gag.

Probably it won't do a lot of good to be too odd, fanciful or
grotesque with murder methods.

The different thing for the villain to be after might be something other than jewels, the stolen bank loot, the pearls, or some other old ones.

Here, again one might get too bizarre.

Unique locale? Easy. Selecting one that fits in with the murder method and the treasure – thing that villain wants – makes it simpler, and it's also nice to use a familiar one, a place where you've lived or worked. So many pulpateers don't. It sometimes saves embarrassment to know nearly as much about the locale as the editor, or enough to fool him.

Here's a nifty much used in faking local colour. For a story laid in Egypt, say, author finds a book titled Conversational Egyptian Easily Learned, or something like that. He wants a character to ask in Egyptian, 'What's the matter?' He looks in the book and finds, 'El khabar, eyh?' To keep the reader from getting dizzy, it's perhaps wise to make it clear, in some fashion, just what that means. Occasionally the text will tell this, or someone can repeat it in English. But it's a doubtful move to stop and tell the reader in so many words the English translation.

The writer learns they have palm trees in Egypt. He looks in the book, finds the Egyptian for palm trees, and uses that. This kids editors and readers into thinking he knows something about Egypt.

Here's the second instalment of the master plot.

Divide the 6000-word yarn into four 1500-word parts. In each 1500-word part, put the following:

FIRST 1500 WORDS

1. *First line, or as near thereto as possible, introduce the hero and swat him with a fistful of trouble. Hint at a mystery, a menace or a problem to be solved – something the hero has to cope with.*

2. *The hero pitches in to cope with his fistful of trouble. (He tries to fathom the mystery, defeat the menace, or solve the problem.)*
3. *Introduce ALL the other characters as soon as possible. Bring them on in action.*
4. *Hero's endeavours land him in an actual physical conflict near the end of the first 1500 words.*
5. *Near the end of first 1500 words, there is a complete surprise twist in the plot development.*

SO FAR:

> *Does it have SUSPENSE?*
> *Is there a MENACE to the hero?*
> *Does everything happen logically?*

At this point, it might help to recall that action should do something besides advance the hero over the scenery. Suppose the hero has learned the dastards of villains have seized somebody named Eloise, who can explain the secret of what is behind all these sinister events. The hero corners villains, they fight, and villains get away. Not so hot.

Hero should accomplish something with his tearing around, if only to rescue Eloise, and surprise! Eloise is a ring-tailed monkey. The hero counts the rings on Eloise's tail, if nothing better comes to mind. They're not real. The rings are painted there. Why?

SECOND 1500 WORDS

1. *Shovel more grief on to the hero.*
2. *Hero, being heroic, struggles, and his struggles lead up to:*
3. *Another physical conflict.*
4. *A surprising plot twist to end the 1500 words.*

NOW:

> *Does second part have SUSPENSE?*
> *Does the MENACE grow like a black cloud?*

Is the hero getting it in the neck?

Is the second part logical?

DON'T TELL ABOUT IT — *show how the thing looked. This is one of the secrets of writing; never tell the reader — show him. (He trembles, roving eyes, slackened jaw, and such.)* MAKE THE READER SEE HIM.

When writing, it helps to get at least one minor surprise to the printed page. It is reasonable to expect these minor surprises to sort of inveigle the reader into keeping on. They need not be such profound efforts. One method of accomplishing one now and then is to be gently misleading. Hero is examining the murder room. The door behind him begins slowly to open. He does not see it. He conducts his examination blissfully. Door eases open, wider and wider, until — surprise! The glass pane falls out of the big window across the room. It must have fallen slowly, and air blowing into the room caused the door to open. Then what the heck made the pane fall so slowly? More mystery.

Characterising a story actor consists of giving him some things which make him stick in the reader's mind. TAG HIM.

BUILD YOUR PLOTS SO THAT ACTION CAN BE CONTINUOUS.

THIRD 1500 WORDS

1. *Shovel the grief on to the hero.*
2. *Hero makes some headway, and corners the villain or somebody in:*
3. *A physical conflict.*
4. *A surprising plot twist, in which the hero preferably gets it in the neck bad, to end the 1500 words.*

DOES:

It still have SUSPENSE?

The MENACE get blacker?

The hero find himself in a hell of a fix?

It all happen logically?

These outlines or master formulas are only something to make you certain of inserting some physical conflict, and some genuine plot twists, with a little suspense and menace thrown in. Without them, there is no pulp story.

These physical conflicts in each part might be DIFFERENT, too. If one fight is with fists, that can take care of the pugilism until next the next yarn. Same for poison gas and swords. There may, naturally, be exceptions. A hero with a peculiar punch, or a quick draw, might use it more than once.

The idea is to avoid monotony.

ACTION:

Vivid, swift, no words wasted.

Create suspense, make the reader see and feel the action.

ATMOSPHERE:

Hear, smell, see, feel and taste.

DESCRIPTION:

Trees, wind, scenery and water.

THE SECRET OF ALL WRITING IS TO MAKE EVERY WORD COUNT.

FOURTH 1500 WORDS

1. Shovel the difficulties more thickly upon the hero.
2. Get the hero almost buried in his troubles. (Figuratively, the villain has him prisoner and has him framed for a murder rap; the girl is presumably dead, everything is lost, and the DIFFERENT murder method is about to dispose of the suffering protagonist.)
3. The hero extricates himself using HIS OWN SKILL, training or brawn.
4. The mysteries remaining – one big one held over to this point will help grip interest – are cleared up in course of final conflict as hero takes the situation in hand.

5.   Final twist, a big surprise (this can be the villain turning out to be the unexpected person, having the 'Treasure' be a dud, etc.)
6.   The snapper, the punch line to end it.

HAS:
  The SUSPENSE held out to the last line?
  The MENACE held out to the last?
  Everything been explained?
  It all happened logically?
  Is the Punch Line enough to leave the reader with that WARM FEELING?
  Did God kill the villain? Or the hero?

*

DO – remember there are taboo subjects in fiction and don't break the taboos. Once upon a time in fiction, savages were noble (unless opposing the British Empire, when they were bloodthirsty), middle-class women were pure, modest, and self-sacrificing, and poor women were clean, honest, hardworking, and devoted to their numerous children. Gentlemen were strong and rational, no one thought about sex and foreigners in Britain were usually a source of trouble.

Ha, ha, we think, we no longer labour under those old restrictions. But, we do.

History

All slaves were aware of their plight and resisted it, all concentration camp victims were noble and all women throughout history have had a strong sense of independence. People crushed, brutalised, beaten down, kept in ignorance, and subjected to unfair discriminatory laws always retained their humanity and self-respect.

By the way, all Frenchmen were in the Resistance and all Londoners cheerful during the Blitz.

In *War and Peace*, Princess Maria Bolkonsky has delayed her escape with her orphaned nephew, as the French troops advance. Asked to pack a wagon for her, the serfs on her estate, who have been drinking, deny there are any horses and wagons available. They do this as they are under the mistaken impression the estate owners are leaving them behind to face the enemy troops. Or perhaps because there are rumours the French conquerors will free the serfs. Meanwhile the Princess is grieving for her lately-dead father and scarcely cares what happens, while her companion, a Frenchwomen, suggests staying on and making a deal with the French when they arrive. The serfs are finally bullied and persuaded to pack a wagon and the Princess escapes. In Tolstoy's novel, the Princess is helpless and the peasants surly behaviour is plainly because they are ignorant, never having had any chance not to be. The scene illustrates the muddle and confusion which occur at times of crisis. But in our modern version, the Frenchwoman might be a spy, the peasants would be led by a calm and reasonable man; they would know the injustice of the state they were living in, and say so, make a few points about serfdom in general and Princess Maria would saddle up, put her nephew in front of her and gallop off, hair streaming behind her, to Moscow.

As the pulp writer is said to have said to the editor, 'Do you want it good or do you want it Tuesday?' The question here is, 'Do you want it true, or do you want it to fit modern conceptions?'

The Present Day

Abortion is the most difficult decision a woman ever makes, foreign residents do not laugh at the British for being dirty, living in dirty houses, undercooking poultry and drinking too much. People with extreme political views whether from right or left cannot lead admirable private lives, no respectable person makes racist or sexist jokes in private and there is nothing fundamentally wrong with our social and political institutions, recycling is virtuous, children a blessing, always loved, money barely exists.

DON'T – rush. 'I'm thirty-five and I haven't had a novel published yet.' One of the best novels of the twentieth century, *The Leopard*, was the first and only novel written by Giuseppe di Lampedusa, then aged fifty-nine. He only did it when his cousin, a poet, won a prize. Convinced he was a better writer than his cousin he wrote his book. Joseph Conrad did not start writing until he was thirty-five. Prior to that he had been a seaman and it was those experiences, not just of where he had been to, but of the men he had met and what he had felt which inform his work.

The reality is that those who take to the pen early and are successful or confident enough to continue to write can lose touch with the wider world. It is not just that their experiences are limited, for a man or a woman can write a significant novel from very limited experience. It is that unless they are very gifted or very lucky their emotional range limits itself, too. We complain that our politicians have never lived 'normal' lives, that they have never done anything but be politicians, but we could make the same complaint about writers who present us with increasingly lame and out-of-touch books about, effectively, themselves and their narrow lives. It's not just a matter of 'using' where you go and who you meet – the dreaded 'material'. It's experience, which may apply itself in many ways. You don't know how useful the life you're leading while waiting to write/finish that novel may be.

DON'T – cough and choke trying to find your 'voice'. The phrase used is 'finding your voice' with its echoes of psychotherapy as in 'finding yourself' of 'finding your inner child' and seems to impose a complicated responsibility on the writer, who is supposed to manage this discovery without even the guidance of a therapist. It's additionally complicated by being an instruction to find what the majority of us were given at birth.

An easier way is to do what most writers do at the outset, take the voice of the writer nearest and dearest to them, the one who has written the book they plan to write themselves and do the same. It's simpler also to think of this missing 'voice' as selecting the best way to tell the story, address the theme from among the myriad of narrative techniques which have grown up since Homer was a boy – when a 'voice' really was a voice, since all stories were spoken or sung.

Writers of fiction are like spies, in the business of conveying information. An authorial voice is the same as an ordinary voice – it informs, entertains, confides, bores, reveals, conceals, alarms and reassures.

If stuck, start with a scene – a girl who has hated the school she's leaving hurls the teacher's parting gift, a book, out of the car, shocking the fellow pupil with her. If you're on a roll, as William Makepeace Thackeray was at the time in *Vanity Fair*, that scene may write itself and you're off to the races.

Otherwise, how to convey what you intend? What must be the longest novel in the English language, Richardson's *Clarissa*, is written entirely in letters. Clarissa writes on strips torn from her garments using soot from the fireplace and so and so forth. She has been abducted and imprisoned but she still keeps up correspondence. In the days when travel was difficult and there were no telephones, letters made sense, but subjective information about events directed to another person – the letters' recipient – is still gripping reading. And emails are letters too; the e-pistolary novel lives!

The undervalued crime writer, George V. Higgins, tells most of his stories through conversations between two people

– two guys in a bar, in a car, talk, talk, talk about this, that and the other. And as we listen to them, the tale emerges. There are diaries – as with letters, the subjective view of one person – there are documents – newspaper cuttings, letters, old manuscripts, records and transcripts, the objective view. Today there is a dearth of musty libraries and attics where trunks still lurk (or that is what we think, except that old paintings and manuscripts continually turn up in them) – but in reality, whether in cellars or attics, cupboards or on computers, our world remains full of records and documents.

It's fun to mix and match, though the technique does have its dangers. In the novels of Wilkie Collins, for example, the straightforward third person narrative, the first person accounts by various characters, the letters and discovered documents can pile up alarmingly, bewildering the reader. Variety is the spice of life, we think – but this? Was the author on drugs? Well yes, he was…

DON'T – worry, be happy. Many of us do things that are demanding and effortful but enjoyable, having children, climbing mountains, surfboarding, playing a musical instrument. Writing can be like this. And it should be.

By the way, DON'T expect action from publishers or agents. Having sent off your book, months – perhaps whole seasons – will elapse before you get an answer, if you get an answer at all. It's easy to get up every morning expecting a response from these powerful individuals but doing that will give you a day filled with the sense of having a lingering and undiagnosable disease. Better to get a grip and decide to complete that loft conversion or OU degree, change your job, get a divorce, move house or adopt a dog.

There are reasons why all this is happening. Once upon a time the process was faster – not fast, but faster. Publishers then were men in cardigans, expected to produce a profit of five-six per cent per annum. The publisher's reader was a clever man or woman, often as not a woman of great taste and literary judgement, held back from running the country by her gender, and the times she lived in. The be-cardiganned man found time to have pub lunches with other becardiganned men while his secretary, wearing a somewhat smaller, brighter cardigan, held the fort and typed at enormous speed. She might have been widowed in World War II. She arrived at 9.30 sharp through fog and hail and was at the office door at 5.30 in her coat. She knew everything. These simple folk had simple titles – 'publisher', 'reader', 'secretary'. Pay was pretty small all round; as someone once remarked: 'An author is a man who has his name in the paper and can't afford to go out to lunch.'

Then came the great takeovers, smaller publishers amalgamated fast into large publishing groups, often owned in the US, Europe or Australia. The publishers became employees in vast corporations. Their obligation was to produce thirteen per cent profit per annum, resulting in economies of scale – higher rewards for some authors, nothing for the many – and publishers and editors in no position to take risks or nurture unprofitable talent until it becomes profitable. Large numbers of people are involved in the decision-making. Caution and slowness prevail. So unless you are a sportsman or sportswoman, a celebrity, related to somebody important or involved in a crime or scandal – don't hold your breath. Just keep your nerve.

The oddness is that while the process in conventional publishing firms seems to have slowed, it is now possible to publish a book online at the touch of a button. That book can reach its potential audience within minutes and be earning its own living by teatime.

It has to be said that writing is an inhuman and unintelligible activity – one must always do it with a certain disdain, without illusions, and leave it to others to believe in one's own work.

Jean Baudrillard

Of all the enemies of literature, success is the most insidious.

Cyril Connolly

It took me fifteen years to discover that I had no talent for writing, but I couldn't give it up because by that time I was too famous.

Robert Benchley

Hilary writes from hard experience, learnt at the coalface. Forty-three years of creating books and getting them published is some achievement. But what is happening now? When I joined the publishing trade the ritual of the 'slush pile' was still a reality. With a strange wink at the language of the ladies of the night, so-called 'unsolicited' manuscripts were allowed through the Goodge Street letter box and dealt with, so long as a stamped and self-addressed envelope was included, with additional postage if the manuscript itself was needed back by the hopeful supplier. And, as with the ritual of removing book wrappers, the job of clearing the pile was usually given to the newest, or youngest member of the editorial staff, for the perception was that little of any worth ever came 'unsolicited'. There were, however, a few manuscripts which made it through. The problem was how much nonsense would be consumed before a worthy manuscript was retrieved from the slush, and how could the process be judged a valuable use of editorial time as more and more of the larger publishing houses began to stop 'unsoliciting' and literary agents began to sprout like weeds across the literary orchard.

It will, we hope, be clear that as well as celebrating the old ways of Grub Street this assortment of elderly book trade anecdotes will point to a few simple truths, but since 'truths' are no longer what they were perhaps we can call them 'rules of the trade'.

In no particular order, here are a few to be going on with:

> *If you want to see the hopeless inefficiency and futility of the capitalist system from the inside, become a publisher. To talk to ninety-five per cent of the booksellers about books is like a nightmare in which you found yourself discussing meat with a butcher who held Shaw's views on meat, meat eating and meat selling.**
> **Leonard Woolf in a letter to Herbert Read, February 1935**

Most booksellers have been incapable of making any useful contribution to the survival of the printed book unless located in white, upper-middle-class enclaves, preferably with some cultural baggage attached – a festival of some sort or location for a television classic serial with a regular source of visitors. And even then, their consistent refusal to source unknown, original or important foreign or home-grown writers is just one reason why Amazon has gazumped their traditional role as cultural gatekeepers.

This inability to take risks, to communicate enthusiasm, to find adventurous new writers or forgotten old ones is a major factor in the inevitable and depressing statistic of bookshop closures. But independents at least can earn brownie points for trying. The wanton destruction of responsible, cooperative bookshop retailing (of which, more later) by the activities of such as the Waterstones chain since its creation has caused more damage to the British publishing trade than any ignorant, stupid independent bookseller could ever have achieved.

---

* Bernard Shaw was a vigorous vegetarian advocate

Technical innovations in the production and distribution of the book, either in printed form or electronic, will always determine what is produced. What the market needs, or what we think it needs, provided as best and cheaply as we can deliver. George Eliot and Charles Dickens probably died before they should have as neither was ever allowed to write the short novels they wanted to. The pressure on George Eliot certainly caused her newly married husband to jump out of the window and Charles Dickens wasn't a barrel of laughs with his children. The lending libraries made too much profit from three-volume novels (three books earn more than one does when subscriptions are paid); the magazines, too much from weekly serialisation and neither of the writers knew about typewriters, let alone computers. Hundreds of pages to be written in pen and ink against ever pressing deadlines, then typeset, then proofread. The typewriter brought some relief, but the computer…that changed everything. A six-hundredodd-page soft-porn gut-buster can be written in a week.

Though there are writers even now who cannot face the screen or the machine's hum, write still in longhand, ink on paper, and in drafts, with each different draft corrected by a different coloured ink. And though the rules can never really help or stop technology's eternal tramp into the unknown, we must surely 'read' a screen differently than we do a book's page and we must surely make books differently. When Kerouac pasted all those pages of foolscap paper together to create an object 'as fat as a kitchen paper-towel roll' which he threw across Robert Giroux's desk,* what might that writer have achieved with an Apple?

In olden Grub Street days, when type was set against typed copy – 'keyed-in' it was called – first proofs were three-foot-long strips of 'galleys'. Each final page was only

---

* The first draft of *On the Road*, rejected by Farrar, Straus & Giroux

set at second proof stage, with proper margins and chapter headings, running heads and terrible financial burdens for authors who changed more than a word or two at what was thought the final stage; when type was set by hand, the cost of moving a reconstructed sentence, created by a nervous author's whim, across on to the next page, or even sometimes the page after that, was significant to any publisher's margins. Now, with 'cut and paste', it's done in seconds. But when mistakes occur, a misplaced comma or adverb missed, no one knows who let it go. In Grub Street days, passing proofs had signatures. A mistake missed first time round or inserted in error on the second proof was not a technological orphan. A human signature had caused it. Now, the printer blames the publisher's electronic file and the publisher blames the author's. And just as in the really olden days when spelling was open to many interpretations and punctuation was personal, the reader handles the 'typos' as best she can.

> *I am always suspicious of a novelist's theories. I have never known them to be anything other than a justification for his own shortcomings.*
> **W. Somerset Maugham**

But maybe now we need a case-study to lighten the load. There's plenty of time to write further of technology or of how Amazon are finally the true answer to the great English bookseller Basil Blackwell's rhetorical question of what is good bookselling: 'Having the right book in the right place at the right time and for the right price.'

So here's Emma Tennant's account of when she was sought after by a mighty American conglomerate, with a starry publisher's editor…what could go wrong?

It's 1991 and the recession is beginning to bite. I'm noticing a cocktail of dumbing down and paying down – accountants at the publishers are staring at unearned balances, and reputations – for being artistic, for having introduced a 'new voice' or style – are about to be shown up for what they are: froth on the daydream, in the unforgettable (and pretentious) words of the French surrealist writer Boris Vian. Everywhere, writers are talking of TV opportunities – or even, as rumour has it that Paramount are about to open an office in London, the true daydream, that of the Hollywood blockbuster. Is the novel dead? Certainly, it appears to have run out of gas; and apart from Martin and Salman, and Bookeritis on the part of editors increasingly glued into conglomerates, there's a flat, weird feeling as culture dies and money, grim reaper of the *literati*, stands in the corner of every room, scythe swinging at the 'lady novelist', the hyper-sensitive or those, in publisher-speak, who were 'badly agented' last time round – i.e. paid a sum their rapidly remaindered book failed to earn back.

What to do? As a fellow writer in the same predicament terms it each time you pay a bill is like breaking off a piece of the fireplace – or cornice – or bedroom door: the house, borrowed against right up to the limit and beyond, is consuming itself in order to keep us all alive. Soon, to pay off the debt, the estate agents will have to be called in – and when the debt *is* paid off, there won't be much more left than the pile of ashes in the hearth. 'He's going to offer,' cries cokehead Bill, as a purchaser stands at the garden gate, flicking his calculator. 'I'll call you later.' But later is already too late.

The phone rings as I'm coming down the stairs of the narrow – but thankfully appreciating in value – little house in Notting Hill. It's a grim day in February, the worst season for showing prospective buyers the property; even if I force the reluctant out into the communal gardens and point at the snowdrops prettily blooming in a Valentine shape on the slight mound I sometimes fantasise as the grave of a previous unsuccessful author, there are more complaints than expressions of admiration. 'What *is* this?' demands a rich Brazilian, pointing upwards at the strange square hole I too have only noticed for the first time, up on the wall next to the French window. The grille, fluttering with cobwebs Mrs Drake's long feather duster has clearly never reached, gives the impression of having featured in a Colditz documentary; as it's cold today it is also painfully evident that February air is entering the sitting-room at liberty. 'What indeed,' I try – but, too late again, the millionaire, as coke king Mike describes him, has already gone. The front door, letting in a blast less inimical than that which I have apparently admitted over the past six years into the centre of my home, has been left insultingly open. Recession makes books and houses, with their vulnerable characters between leaves or storeys, and their ability to go out of fashion overnight, into tragic siblings.

'Is this Emma?' The voice is low; and if not exactly husky, somehow familiar in its 'I'm speaking very softly because I'm incognito' timbre. Can it be Lauren Bacall? But I don't know Lauren Bacall; and even though I have a script for a vampire film under consideration at the BBC, I somehow doubt the famous Betty Bacall would be cold-calling me for a part in it. But – where on earth have I heard this voice – American, obviously and 'thrilling'? 'This is Jacqueline Onassis,' the voice says.

'Oh HELLO,' I hear myself replying with a sort of desperate heartiness. The saying that if you throw enough mud at the wall some of it is bound to stick comes back to me as I struggle for composure in the face of this unlikely communication from the far side of the Atlantic, and as I try to remember which piece of writing I sent in that direction – portion and outline, as the submission of a synopsis and a supposedly exciting sample chapter is termed in the trade – a whole host of embarrassments present themselves. Was my casually aimed mud pie a nerve-tinglingly erotic follow-up to Jane Austen's *Persuasion*, with girls leaping in their calico and bonnets from the cob at Lyme Regis into the arms of a dashing captain? Or was it *Memoirs of a Corgi*, a brisk satire on Court life and the royal marriage? No, that would surely not be sufficiently American, for the firm of Doubleday, whence my caller spoke so compellingly. Well then – could it be – 'You mention HUGH,' the voice came low and penetrating into my ear. 'You knew him? You knew Hugh?'

Of course. I feel relief, accompanied by a sick dread that I may actually have to write the book I outlined. My own family: this had been the subject, the title too shaming even to begin to recall. I'd done a portion – or had I? Visions of the green and purple hills of my childhood home in the Borders of Scotland, rendered in prose similar in hue, rose in front of me and then thankfully faded away. Surely, the limp and boring offering that was my 'book about my family' couldn't possibly interest anyone in the vibrant, modern US of A? And, of all people, the 'editor' who now hung on the line, breathy and expectant, for my reply. 'Yes I knew Hugh,' I said, like an automaton. And, upping the stakes despite myself – 'he was a cousin. Hugh was the son of Laura, daughter of…'

My voice tails away, as the circumstances of this painful submission return with full force. A table at a restaurant in Fulham Road swims into view…a man with a cheerful, impish expression tucking into haddock fishcakes…and Decca, Jessica Mitford, lighting up her fiftieth mentholated cigarette and warming to her theme. (If there's trouble, you can bet there's a Mitford in there somewhere.) 'SUCH a good idea,' Decca – as she was invariably known – cries, and her husband the fishcake-eater Bob Treuhaft nods enthusiastically. 'We'll ask Renee Golden – she's the agent, well she's an attorney but I keep forgetting and calling her an agent, to sell it for you. You'll be HUGELY rich in no time at all.' 'Your family,' Bob concurs – though I don't know why this was the first of my projects which came to mind. 'Renee will sell it – make no mistake about that.' 'Don't leave out the Princess Margaret bits,' Decca puts in, brisk and businesslike as usual. 'Yanks love royalty. Make her a secret spy or something.' 'I was going to write about the Industrial Revolution,' I said lamely. 'My great-grandfather more or less invented chlorine, you see.' 'The Americans will never have heard of your family,' Bob says as a plate of summer pudding is dumped before him. 'Yes, Renee will MAKE people excited,' Decca agrees, 'even if they've never heard of one they do love Hitler and the Queen and all that sort of thing.'

Now, at any rate, someone has heard of Hugh, I reflect, as the scarlet of my first reaction to the telephone call drains from my face, to be replaced by a ghastly pallor I can see in the mirror over the table where I stand, attached by the phone cord to the most famous woman in the world. They may not know about the Industrial Revolution – or even care about Stalin or Hitler or the Queen – but Hugh, they've heard of him. 'I LOVED Hugh!' sighs the voice which seems now to have become no more than a wisp of vapour rising from the underworld. 'And he's your cousin. This is going to be such a wonderful, wonderful book.' 'Oh, so you' – I stutter into the black Bakelite receiver, its surface now greasy with my anxiety and sweat. 'You've read…' 'I think your grandmother was a fascinating and beautiful woman,' Jackie – am I really allowed to call her that? – says, and, vain as are most writers,

I feel a surge of love for the woman I now see to be the most discerning – and sadly underrated – editor in the business. 'If…' I say humbly, my vision of the subtle and profound work on which I am to embark now releasing a cloud of reckless happiness, 'if I could possibly make the book a little bit personal? I mean, rather than just a history of…of the Industrial Revolution…' 'YES, YES.' The respiratory sounds accompanying my new employer's enthusiasm led me to wander whether a recent photograph of Hugh, seen exiting from the Ritz Hotel at 4 am on the occasion of Mrs Onassis's visit to London, had really signified what Hugh himself had announced widely, a night of passion and delight, or had in fact been an evening discussing the old times when Jack had been alive, as the newspapers rather primly had reported. 'You should be personal,' the voice said – and, like an auditory equivalent of the Cheshire Cat's grin, it lingered, after an unmistakable click. Jackie had rung off. She wanted my book to be as 'personal' as I desired. I was Marcel Proust – or the author I much admired, depicter of family scenes both invented and true, Sybille Bedford. Decca – and through her, the mysterious Renee Golden – had brought me fame and fortune. I was made.

Renee Golden – who announced later that evening that she was arriving shortly in London from LA and would like me to put her up (my aunt obliged in the end) – could be heard rattling bangles on the metal her name describes, as she spoke with a crisp excitement into my exhausted ear. 'I've had a good conversation with Jackie…' she began. And she went on to assure me my holiday problems were now distinctively at an end. 'You'll summer at Hyannisport no doubt. And wistfully – right up to Labor Day.'

*

I've been writing my Family Book for some time now, and sending wodges of it to Jackie at Doubleday. Although I'm grateful to her in the extreme for saying I can make the book as 'personal' as I like – and thus consider her almost the perfect recipient of the reminiscences-cum-family-history now taking shape on the page – I've noticed I tend to keep quiet when people ask me who I'm actually writing this *for*. 'Jacqueline Onassis, as it happens' can bring sniggers, even contemptuous comments; in the case of Mr McLaren, the Bank Manager, the hearty tone of his early morning harassment call is tinged with disbelief, of an 'If you're writing a book for Jackie Onassis I'm signed up by the Queen of the Fairies' variety. This is enough to engender a massive writer's block – though I know there's no such thing as a block taken as a reason for failure to pay the interest charges of the Bank of Scotland.

In that half-waking state so important to writers – that time before the first cup of tea and Mr McLaren's early morning call, which, like the purple heather prose I'm producing for Jackie, is always in too broad a Scots to sound convincing ('I'm no fretting the day: I'll gie ye till Monday') – I find I'm fantasising about the great good fortune my new editor will bring me. Instead of planning a morning describing the ancestors showing their mettle, inventing bleach or striding about on the moors brought as a result of the chemical success of the white powder, I'm giving Jackie the chance to extricate me from the bog my professional life has landed me in. 'Hi, this is Jacqueline Onassis,' I hear the soft breathy voice begin. 'Is this Jock McLaren? I've heard so much about you…' But before I can go on, I wake properly and stagger out of bed to go and put the kettle on. An 'ordinary' run-of-the-mill publisher might be prepared to call their author's bank and substantiate the coming of the advance. A reputable British agent might be able to do the same. But Renée Golden, despite her promising name, has failed to impress Mr McLaren. For one thing, as Decca had informed me, she is an attorney and not an agent, living in LA and thus puzzlingly far removed from the world of New York publishing; for another, the doughty Renée has over-praised me to the cautious Scot, and her assurances that this book will be a mega-mega have made him all the more doubtful of my veracity. A book on my family? Didn't a close relative recently call on Mr McLaren with a photograph of his pet elephant – the beast a rarity on the remote island to which it had been transported – and point proudly to the leather bags, these resembling satchels worn by bus conductors in the Fifties, which were attached to the animal's flanks. Pennies garnered from the locals in return for a ride on the elephant, apparently filled these receptacles, and McLaren was now expected to increase his applicant's borrowing when confronted by this visible proof of income. It was all very well to cite an ancestor, Sir Charles, who appeared to have invented the overdraft in the mid-nineteenth century, by speaking cannily to the newly formed Bank. Sir Charles had gone on to make a success of his business life. But I had a sinking feeling that my efforts were placed by the manager and his colleagues on a par with the elephant. Why on earth should Mr McLaren – or, come to that, the Head of the Bank of Scotland (I sometimes fantasised him, kilted and superb, as he came down from the Mound in Edinburgh, a radiant Jackie on his arm. All my troubles would be solved by their coming together, I reflected bitterly) – why should any of them want anything further to do with my now decadent and collapsing family? Little wonder there was surprise at the assertion that Mrs Onassis was keen enough on the idea to commission a tome on the uninspiring subject.

*

45

The phone rings. There has been a long period of silence from the offices of Doubleday – or the yacht hung with Renoirs and Toulouse-Lautrecs where I read of her on occasion, late summer sun combated by the blackest of dark glasses – or indeed Hyannisport, where Renée Golden, deep in her own imagining, has placed Jackie and myself in eternity. I am writing to my own satisfaction: my grandmother, a 'famous beauty', was not unlike the fascinating – and self-fascinated – widow of the late President, I conclude: like Jacqueline Kennedy Onassis, she loved to encourage the adoration of the world while insisting on seclusion and total privacy. I'm pondering on history's cruellest trick, its inability to give an idea of how people spoke – was my grandmother's voice quiet, almost ghostly but with a troublingly sexual undertow, like Jackie? – when I lift the receiver unthinkingly. And I hear those cadences, as unmistakable as Mr McLaren's (it's evening, explaining my rash approach to the telephone; I know to the minute when the Bank Manager goes home, to oversee, as he sometimes laughingly informs me, the maths homework of his daughter Amanda). 'Is this Emma?' comes the voice that pauses and swoops like a swallow, waits for its moment of revelation and then falls into a swoon of non-saying, of a listening silence that encourages the maddest of confidences. 'I just want to say what a wonderful description of landscape you have written – around your home in…in…' 'Scotland,' I answer, the crimson unrolling like a strip of ceremonial carpet up from my neck to my cheeks. How clever, how discerning, of this woman who for all her sophistication and world travel is after all not English, let alone Scottish, to appreciate my descriptive powers. But here I begin to wonder, did they meet on the moors, Jackie and Hugh? – am I, by writing this Rob Roy portrait of the Borders, providing her only with fond memories? Writers' vanity, an affliction far worse than block, overcomes me. 'I'm glad you like it,' I say modestly.

It takes me at least three or four minutes to understand that Jackie is trying to tell me something else altogether. The long and short of it is that she – or maybe someone else high up at the publisher's office – doesn't like my efforts so far at all. The book is meant to be a *history* of my family. The famous voice goes down a few more octaves and then does its disappearing-under-the-bedclothes act. I can hear only faint sighs and moans in the ensuing silence. I clear my throat, as if this brisk sound can somehow rise to hit the satellite – or dash about in cables buried deep in the Atlantic sea, wherever it does go to connect us to our calls to the United States of America – and clear up both Jackie's larynx and the misunderstanding, as I see it must be, over the nature of my book. 'And when you write of your grandmother Pamela,' the manatee's subaqueous whisper recommences as I stand in my first floor kitchen looking out on an autumnal evening, leaves on the chestnut trees dying along with my hopes for a sum that will satisfy Mr McLaren – 'when you write of her casket…' 'She called her children her jewels,' I say in a strangled voice, almost as inaudible as Jackie's. If they hate the book over there, what on earth difference does my grandmother, as I described her (metaphorically and whimsically as I now see) opening her casket to unfold her adored children, make to their overall dislike of my 'personal' account of my family? 'Casket means coffin to me,' Jackie's voice soughs in the branches of the trees. A new silence ensues; there has been a murmur to say good-bye – or was that the equinoctial gale outside building up with the aim of removing the tiles once more from the roof, just a few feet above my bed at the top of the house?

Whichever way, I spend the evening in a silence almost equal to Jackie's. How could she not like the opening of my Family Book, with its sharp, sardonic portrait of a dinner in 1911? Easily, the voice of truth answers from inside me. It's deadly boring, that's why.

It takes me some hours and conversations with friends to come to terms with the fact that (a) the first chapters will have to be rewritten; and (b) there is at the top of the contract (I hadn't bothered to read it) a small paragraph spelling out the expected content of the Family Book. There is nothing personal mentioned therein. 'So you don't have a leg to stand on,' one of my more down-to-earth friends remarks.

The night which follows this debacle is on a par with the storm which rages outside. The tiles and slates tumble merrily from the roof just above my head as the visions return: the casket; Jackie; old film footage of the assassination of JFK. The shame and horror – how *could* I have used the word 'casket?' Surely I knew it would awaken terrible memories for my poor editor – are intercut with my own insignificant but real horrors of the coming day. How can I write the very book I'd said I didn't want to write? – namely, a history – without feeling or personal reminiscence of my own family? How could I not have understood what they really wanted? Do they even know themselves?

I lie awake until the great winds subside, and under my stripped roof I wake again immediately to await McLaren's promised call.

*

Autumn of 1992: trees in the communal gardens seem bare earlier than usual, conkers seized prematurely by boys from young, rich families who have come to settle here, hoping for the fake rustic idyll increasingly denied by recession and the effects of the Gulf War. Missiles aimed at anyone who tries to circumnavigate the muddy patch that once was grass suitable for the Filipino-served banquets hosted by these international millionaires, and with disconcerting accuracy bang on the head: acorns from pea shooters, chestnuts still in their spiky armour, even (until confiscated) an air rifle, which shoots right through my sitting-room window as I sit trying to compose a letter to Mr McLaren.

The struggle to satisfy Jackie is on a par with the bright, frightening images on TV of conflict and its ambiguous results. Am I writing the kind of thing she will like, once the personal has been taken out? Does the fact of my great-grandfather putting up the tallest chimney in the world, higher than the Pyramids even, seem likely to turn her on? I falter, run out of ammunition; finally, after four months I give up in despair and fax her with the news that I can't see myself going on with the book. The Glasgow chimney subsides; the ghost of my grandmother, waiting in the wings to be reintroduced to the story, fades in the morning light. I know now: I wasn't meant to write about my family this way. Unless, a voice murmurs from the pile of Bank correspondence on my work table, you pull yourself together and find a new, cleaner and clearer way. After all, it's an interesting story. Or is it? – the other voice says, as the spoiled scion of an industrial giant tours the garden, ghetto blaster in hand. If I complain, another bullet hole may deter buyers from offering on the perpetually-for-sale house. '*It's going to be a wonderful book,*' another ghostly voice, that of Jackie herself, whispers over the dementing rock.

That was about all that came from my editor over the Family Book – except for a friendly call once I had resigned from the job. 'We'll start our courtly dance' came the breathy tones. And – as Renée Golden reported the next day, 'She said you were wonderful.' So, apart from knowing how wonderful my book might have been, and how wonderful I am after having failed to deliver – exactly where do I stand? What is the courtly dance and how does it end? 'With you flat on your back,' the inevitable friend remarks.

By March some of my 'gumption' – a word I shall learn to dread later when attempting, equally foolishly, to satisfy an American publisher with a replay of *Gone with the Wind* – returns to me and I decide to try with the Family Book again. 'Just write it,' other bored and exhausted authors snap at me: sympathy for my predicament is rapidly running out. 'For God's sake, start at the beginning and go on until the end. And do a new outline. That'll pacify them.'

And so it did – though the courtly dance turned out to be more of a game of musical chairs than a quadrille, in the end. My new outline was as clean and clear as anyone could have hoped for, and Jackie accepted it. But – and there seemed to be steps involved in this dance which I simply hadn't learned – the book was cancelled anyway. The new delivery date was declared unacceptable. Jackie wrote to Renée saying, 'Books have life of their own and this one seems to have ended. I suspect it will come as a great relief to Emma.'

Jackie: The Payback

I'm geared up for publication of the Book About My Family that's taken such an age – and gone through so many possible editors and publishers – when a bolt comes out of the blue. The sky in fact is blue, it's a fine April day, and primroses are out in the lanes near our (McLaren-borrowed) cottage in Dorset. Everything seems to be going well: a host of interviews have taken place and are beginning to appear in the press; and an early review in *The Times* describes me as charming. I'm pleased with myself, and thankful I was able to write the book I wanted to write.

So when I'm back in London and the call comes from Dan Franklin, my editor at Cape, I am at first unable to take in its meaning. Surely…surely they can't stop my Sebald-inspired account of my family over the past century… Surely…but it turns out, as far as Doubleday, original 'Jackie' publishers of what I know myself to be quite a different book, there is definitely no mistake. On the day preceding publication they have threatened Cape – and thus Random House – with an injunction if they go ahead and publish *Strangers: A Family Romance*. The Book About My Family for Doubleday, unwritten and abandoned for over five years due, in my view, to a total failure of communication between JKO and myself, turns out to be a landmine, activated by Cape's publication of my memoir.

The editor's voice is commendably even and friendly – for it cannot be pleasant, after months of work line-editing, making useful suggestions and the rest – to find your effort is in line for a quick pulping. Not to mention the money: cost of production and advance, long ago swallowed by McLaren, to the author. Book already in catalogue, even subject of review and interviews.

I confess this sort of thing inclines me to the madly impractical. 'You should have read the short paragraph in the front of your contract with Doubleday,' says one friend when I've rummaged in papers still suffering from multiple house moves, dog-eared and missing vital components. 'Look, it says here that you'll write a history of your family, not an impressionistic portrait of yourself or your grandmother.' 'Perhaps I could change their names,' I go on wildly. 'I mean, readers here could be given the nod by a kind of coded reference in the blurb, that this novel featuring people called, say, Eliot, was really a book about my family.' 'Don't be silly,' the friend reasonably said.

It seemed there was no way out. Jackie's death, I admit, had had the effect of freeing me, or so I thought, from any further claims by the once prospective publishers of *The Chemistry of Money*, a title appealing both to Jackie Onassis and Renée Golden. Unfairly – as I came to see it to be – I'd decided the whole exercise had been bound up with a possible infatuation with Hugh – and had passed, very likely – when a better-starred romance turned up. 'Offer them something else,' said my friend, now as far off the mark as I had just shown myself to be. 'You could do a biography of Princess Margaret. Then you wouldn't have to pay back all those dollars.'

Even the mention of a sum of this dimension is inclined to bring on an attack of McLarenitis and I cross the room to pick up the phone to the estate agents, these, like the literary agents in my long and heroic campaign to keep the show on the road, inclined to be cautious at the sound of my voice at the other end of the wire. 'You asked us last week to value the property,' the 'Chief Negotiator' at Winkworth, or Foxtons, or Marsh & Parsons, replies tiredly. 'You were going to come back to us about the subsidence problem.' 'Oh GOD, the subsidence problem,' I cry as I ring off, my impassioned plea for help coinciding with the continuing drone of the friend's insistence I give the US publisher a life of Princess Margaret. 'Why, what IS her subsidence problem?' my companion goes on, alarmed. 'Oh, for heaven's sake.' 'You could even do the Queen Mother, at a pinch.'

Later, as I stand by the window overlooking what is described by a neighbouring writer and historian as the 'seedy end of the street', I distinctly feel the floor sloping more vertiginously than it had done only a few days before. It's true, the houses here in the suddenly fashionable Notting Hill were deserted by the sensible rich when their lack of foundations became evident. Now only the daft rich go for them (but not now, of course, not now). There's a recession in more ways than one; in the hysteria incurred by the threat of my new book being 'disappeared' by the Americans I feel the house actually recede as well as do a Titanic into the dog-shit-littered crescent. Soon the little craft will go under altogether, only the debt to McLaren remaining (the most recent bank statement acting as a cautionary flag).

The general craziness of money came to mind as I signed an agreement promising to give all US royalties in another book, to the publisher. 'A pal of mine worked in the same firm as Jackie,' Decca's voice returns to me from the days when her phone calls and airmail letters from California cheered me on in my endeavours and Renée Golden assured me I would prosper as Decca just had after signing up for a book and going on holiday: 'She and Bob returned yesterday rested, refreshed and RICH.' 'The pal who worked alongside Jackie,' Decca said, 'had just one big worry about her. D'you want to know what it is?' I said I did; Decca was a tease all her life and I braced myself for a possibly revolting revelation. 'She said it was great fun working alongside Mrs Onassis. But she couldn't understand how she managed to dress so well on the editor's salary...' And Decca laughs and laughs.

So that was that. I cannot say whether I believe a good and interesting book would have resulted from my new outline. But I knew that a true miscommunication had taken place between Doubleday and myself – and that their demands for repayment, repeated at intervals over the years, didn't seem fair to me. Perhaps, as Renée, now bravely relinquishing the Hyannisport dream for ever, suggested in a note shortly after, they had simply decided they didn't want the book any more. Perhaps Jackie sensed my difficulty in writing about my family without including myself in the narrative and believed the new book – accepted by her – wouldn't really work. It is impossible to come to any firm conclusion. Meanwhile, a raw spring of 1993 sets in. 'I'm afreet for ye,' McLaren says with a touch of warmth and concern in his voice. 'It's the interest rates, ye ken...' 'I'll think of something,' I say.

In Ian Norrie's *Mentors and Friends*, when he wrote of André Deutsch, he recalled an incident at his beloved Garrick Club whilst hosting a small dinner party he gave there to celebrate the launch of one of his London anthologies, published by Deutsch:

> André became distantly polite when we met. Giles Gordon, my agent, had pushed him to a larger advance than I actually wanted by calling him mean. I asked George Mikes [then one of Deutsch's more successful authors] why André was being unfriendly. George replied promptly, 'You must be losing him money.'

Norrie also remembered, in his memoir of Christina Foyle in the same volume, that her *Commonplace Book*, which she had kept for most of her life, was also published by André Deutsch: 'In a section entitled, The Conduct of a Business, she quotes H. P. Kraus (antiquarian bookseller) from whom she learned: "Never leave employees alone and presume they're working."'

A certain meanness of spirit always hovers in the shadows of any true bookman or woman's mind. Envy at the success of others, a terror of the workhouse (or the twenty-first century equivalent) and delight in a rival's failure are just three manifestations. And though we know we cannot help our feelings but we can help what we do with them, the new ways of communication have tended to sanitize the creative power of bad behaviour. Would Emma's tale have been quite the same if Jackie O had email? But perhaps we need a few more anecdotes from the bad old days before extending that argument.

Norrie, once more, on another Grub Street legend, Stanley Unwin:

> Sir Stanley's alleged meanness was legendary in the book trade. His family report on it... Philip [his son] is precise: 'His frugality ... extended to such little things as the famous stubs of pencil with which he did all his writing.' David [his eldest son – Stanley was an epic traveller, maintaining he was an ambassador for the British book trade, thereby ensuring the British Council in any city he visited would both meet him at the airport and provide a government car – on a trip to the Far East] found himself expected to cut costs by sharing a bedroom with father. He resolved this situation by keeping a fan whirring all night until the old man finally booked separate rooms. From Japan he wrote...to his wife: 'He has nearly a thousand pounds here...in blocked currency but is reluctant to use taxis even in Tokyo and will walk miles rather than spend 100 yen (.../-)... I was reprimanded for being over hasty in purchasing a newspaper it turned out we didn't want. Cost: not quite twopence. ("Ah, but you've never had difficulty in earning a few pence, etc.") He should be made to tear up and throw away at least five pounds daily...'

Allen & Unwin exist now only as an independent publishing firm in Australia and New Zealand, no bad thing to be perhaps when you consider what happened to the mother country's imprints.

In 1986, Allen & Unwin merged with Bell & Hyman, forming the company, Unwin Hyman, purchased four years later by Rupert Murdoch's News International's HarperCollins. HarperCollins cherry-picked the best goodies, like J. R. R. Tolkein, and flogged what had become the Unwin Hyman academic division to Thomson Books' Routledge division (note the introduction of military/football jargonese, superseding 'imprint'). Routledge and Kegan Paul, another venerated English publisher, whose Bloomsbury offices were almost next to George Allen & Unwin, had been slaughtered in 1985, merging with Associated British Publishers (one of the first home-cloned conglomerates, formed to counter the increasing power of American academic publishers in the late 1950s, created from yet more venerated, old publishing names such as Methuen and Chapman & Hall). Parts of ABP (as it came to be called) had been sold to the Thomson group in 1987, who then formed its Routledge division, which, after a management buyout in 1996, backed by venture capital, was sold in 1998 to the Taylor & Francis Group (another venerated English publisher founded in 1852). Phew!

The Taylor & Francis Group merged with Informa plc in 2004, a multinational group that, according to its website, provides: 'academics, businesses and individuals with unparalleled knowledge, up-to-the minute information and highly specialist skills and services. With around 7,000 employees working in some 150 offices in over 40 countries, our global reach and breadth of offer is unique.' Its managing director in 2012 was paid a bonus of 1,225,700 Swiss francs, but so far I've been unable to discover his spending habits on foreign trips. Maybe that's only justice, given how Stanley Unwin never paid Bertrand Russell (now a jewel in Informa's crown) an advance (if Ian Norrie's account is reliable): Philip Unwin (Sir Stanley's nephew who worked closely with the old man and was responsible for discovering Thor Heyerdahl, whose *Kon-Tiki Expedition* is still filling Murdoch's coffers) 'supposed he was behaving correctly in giving the author a four-figure advance'. According to Norrie, Bertrand Russell delivered a new book in person whilst Sir Stanley was abroad;

on being given the cheque 'Russell was pleasantly surprised; Sir Stanley's reaction is not recorded'.

It was the agent Andrew Wylie who defended, and demanded, the payment of huge advances in order to force publishing conglomerates to take their investments seriously: the logic was that if you've spent a large dollop of cash, you're more likely to work hard to get it back, and if you don't, tough luck. Looking after the pennies in order to garner the pounds just isn't the same. A Wylie not speaking is the very opposite of an André Deutsch not speaking to an Ian Norrie; agents don't speak to publishers now when the advances don't earn out on the sum demanded as an advance was agreed.

Detectives always say 'follow the money' as they attempt to solve the murder. And maybe I've been skirting round the subject of money with old Grub Street tales of meanness and stubborn eccentricity. Perhaps one more tale of Sir Stanley Unwin might finally show my drift.

When another Thor Heyerdahl book, *The Ra Expeditions*, was published in 1972, Claude Gill Books was offered a six-foot scale model of the papyrus boat in which the intrepid Viking had sailed across the Atlantic. Allen & Unwin made it a condition that we ordered three hundred and fifty copies, or else the spectacular model would go off to Harrods. After some intense negotiation, they agreed a small additional discount on the standard discount, a third off the published price, then the norm with Allen and Unwin, and with many other general trade publishers. Sir Stanley's well publicised view on not increasing discounts was his cost in maintaining an expensive distribution centre in Hemel Hempstead which provided a next day delivery (which was true – it did). A bookseller need not tie-up her money in slow-moving stock or deny any customer his order tomorrow, thus confidently taking a cash deposit or even, after a phone call to check availability, cash in advance. Thus, by diligent and intelligent stock control, any bookseller, anticipating a thirty-day sales cycle for Sir Stanley's books and paying against a monthly statement, should never have to invest unsustainable amounts in dead stock. And since it was widely believed that *The Ra Expeditions* would be the number-one Christmas bestseller, combined with the spectacular model in the shop's window, we should be grateful for the additional two and a half per cent. And that was his last word on the subject.

All went well to begin with. It was indeed a splendid scale model. One always knew how successful a window display was by the number of fingerprints which had appeared overnight, when the window was cleaned in the morning. *Ra* was well up to standard. The worry was that the book was not the success that had been foretold. The publisher did take back around one hundred copies when the display was dismantled and the model removed but when finally Christmas came and went and we prepared to get ready for the annual January stocktake, Allen and Unwin refused, on Sir Stanley's instructions, to take back the rest of the unsold books. As we argued, the relationship became frosty, culminating in the publisher's warehouse closing our account as two large piles of *Ra* stood unsold in a corner of the ground-floor shop and the invoice for the two hundred and fifty copies at a one-third discount, plus two and a half per cent, was left unpaid.

It could not rest there, however, as Allen & Unwin also published *The Hobbit* and other assorted Tolkiens and Bertrand Russell, whose autobiography and one-volume history of Western philosophy were then constant bestsellers. It would be inconceivable that a large London West End bookseller would not have them in stock, so once again the family-run wholesaler, Bertram Books, was called upon to do the dirty. When Sir Stanley realised he was giving more away, as the wholesale discount was far greater than the bookshop one, a face-saving all round compromise was negotiated. Bertram's were no longer needed.

Elsie Bertram had set up a small paperback wholesale business catering to the Norfolk holiday trade supplying popular holiday potboilers from her chicken shed and making a buck or two, as her son was a salesman for Pan Books, then the main, brash rival to the ubiquitous Penguin Books. Her fortune was assured when Paul Hamlyn's warehouse was blacklisted by the print unions in 1968. He offered Elsie extended credit, subsidised her additional logistic costs to provide enough transport to break the strike and Bertram's distributed his books nationwide. She never looked back. The family business sold in 1999, she and her family made millions (though their loyal staff, it must be noted, were given some of the loot), and after a choppy ride culminating in the bankruptcy of the Woolworth group (who had bought the wholesaler some years after that first sale) Bertram's became part of Smiths News plc, a public company with an annual report and director remunerations as thick and pretty as Informa plc.

And Bertram's demand that they can return every unsold copy of any book they've ever ordered from publishers within eighteen months of the initial order, at discounts of over fifty per cent of the published price. If the money's followed, the merge and mash of buying and selling publishing imprints and retail book outfits has been often subsidised by the wanton demands of greedy retailers who demand no responsibility for failure to sell whatever they order.

What would Sir Stanley make of that? The Grub Street we all walked down was elitist. It was certainly snobbish. Unwin's autobiography, *The Truth about a Publisher*, is exact:

> Making money, I can truthfully say, has never presented any difficulty to me. I could have been a

millionaire had that been my objective in life; but that is nothing of which to be proud. I always agreed with my craftsmen brother Bernard when he rubbed into me that 'the trick of making money out of almost anything was a special gift of very doubtful moral value'... It cannot be too highly emphasised that publishers are not dealing with a mere commodity like soap or soda, where the advantages of mass production are overwhelming, but with the lively offspring of an author's mind. In a publisher... the recognition that he is *not* dealing with a mere commodity, but handling his sensitive and suspicious authors' children, each with an individuality of his own, is the beginning of wisdom. It is this factor which dictates the optimum size of a publisher's business, beyond which it is inexpedient to go.

Sir Stanley wrote this 1960, a few years before I started in the trade and only half a century before Jeff Bezos would start up Amazon in his mother's garage, yet it could be a voice from before the Battle of Waterloo.

The destruction of the publisher as a cultural force with clout is well told by the tale of two feminist imprints. But just before that's begun, let's see what was happening not many years after Sir Stanley's edict on publishing power.

Hilary wrote an article on Feminist Writing for *Bananas* in the summer of 1977...

THE MISERABILISTS
A NEW GENRE
Hilary Bailey

I had intended to begin writing by using what some shagged-out journalists may still be calling a 'snappy opening'. Four out of ten women admitted to mental hospitals in 1976 had tried to slash their wrists with the end papers of *The Golden Notebook* is the sort of thing I mean. Instead I wish, humbly and dully, to say that while reading many books by women novelists, from Barbara Cartland (*Sweet Punishment*, 1931) to Margaret Drabble (*The Realms of Gold*, 1975), although normally of a robust constitution, I became ill. Headaches, fever and lassitude accompanied my labours. I became, in short, a Victorian heroine, vapourish and no doubt on the verge of brain fever. Leaving off, I felt better. Starting to read again, I felt the symptoms come back. This time one eye – probably the softer and more feminine one – gushed mucus, in sympathy. The other, perhaps governed by the animus, remained beady and, if depressed, still dry. No stranger to what I conceive of, now, as a new genre in fiction – I have made my own contribution to it and may well do so again – I feel unashamed about recording the effect these books, en masse, had on me. And I shall reveal why.

> She walked, in the noise of traffic past the overflowing dustbins in the basements, through the rainy streets, where a watery light cast itself over the cars and buses going by. A man hurried out of the bank. The old lady, whose name she did not know, walked ahead of her on bent legs, plimsolls on her feet.
> 'Hullo. How are you?'

'You know my hamster. It died. I found it on its back in the morning, in its cage, with its legs stuck up in the air. It gets cold at night in that room when the fire dies down.'

The child whose hand she held tugged impatiently. 'I want to go home. Why do we have to go there? I want to go home and ride my bicycle.'

She looked down at him. 'Not far now.'

They reached the large municipal building on the corner and went inside.

When she got home, the telephone was ringing. He said, 'Actually,' and, passing, said again, 'actually, I'm living in South Kensington at present.' As he spoke, with his voice seeming strangely far away, she looked down at the table, noticing for the first time the telegram about her mother, which had been propped up, for her to see, against the teapot, among the dirty cups.

This is my own attempt to produce the tone and some of the areas covered by the genre. It is in fact an account, apart from the telegram, of my own visit to the public library a few weeks ago. A more controlled writer might have had the self-discipline to leave out the passage about the hamster, or replace the poor animal with something more respectable, such as a dog or a child, but if the reader spots this as a lapse, a bit of faulty artistic selection, then that is additional proof that we are inside a genre, with its own expectations, conventions and respectabilities. What, then, can be seen in this invented passage which looks typical of a number of other books? Not much is happening; nevertheless the telephone call and the telegram hint that trouble is coming from the outside. As far as the actual outside is concerned, it is grubby and neutral, if not actually inimical – the traffic hurries past, the building is large and alien. The woman has no part in either of them, as a traveller or a ratepayer. Her world is the slow walk with an old woman and a small child through this landscape which has nothing to do with her. She, the child and the old woman are all nameless, distanced. And the woman, part of the action, and its focus, initiates nothing and reacts to nothing. It is always as if everything were happening to her. So we sense, through the unwashed cups, the passivity and the lack of response, that she is in a bad way, perhaps because of an event, perhaps because of life itself. Above all, we are examining, not happenings, but the subject's experience of them. The eyes through which we see everything are the eyes of the author/character, for there is no pretence that the main character does not stand for the author. If such books are not autobiographical in terms of the action, they are in terms of the main character – her ideas, responses and sensibility. The question is further complicated by the fact that the books deal with the matter of most women's lives so that this 'I-she' character is also the personage with whom the reader, most usually a woman, is most likely to identify itself. So there is a way in which these novels are a kind of sharing and exposing of experience, as other novels are not. They are like two women discussing a third, who, say, is having trouble with a child, an erring husband or trying to decide whether to have her old mother to live with the family or not. They know the problem. They know how they have dealt with it and on this sympathetic basis they judge, criticise and predict. And this, I am sure, is one of the reasons for the popularity of the genre – it is less fiction than an analysis of the condition of being a woman.

How did this happen? I believe that in the late 1950s and early 60s a handful of seminal books, very different in some ways, very alike in others, were published. They claimed a territory, set a style and established the proposition that books by women, about themselves, could be taken seriously. It is no coincidence that they appeared at a time when appeals for liberty by oppressed groups inside society – the young, blacks, women – were becoming louder and stronger. The books I am talking about were *The Golden Notebook* by Doris Lessing (1962), *The Bell Jar* by Sylvia Plath (1963), *The Dud Avocado* by Elaine Dundy (1958), *The Pumpkin Eater* by Penelope Mortimer (1962), and *The Country Girls* by Edna O'Brien (1960). To this list I might well add Nell Dunn's reportage book, *Up the Junction* (1963). They are very different books with different qualities,* but each of these books, all published within five years of each other, will be familiar to people who read novels; all are, so far as I know, still in print and widely sold in their paperback versions. I doubt if there is a woman writer working today who will not have read most of them. They started a tradition. There is not one book among them where women do not predominate. The tales are always told in the first person, or in that 'I-she' personage already mentioned. The men in the books are always seen in their romantic relationship to the main character. At their best these men are merely stupid, insensitive and incompetent – when the heroine of *The Bell Jar*'s first sexual experience ends in dangerous haemorrhage the man in the case proves inadequate. At their worst they are rotten, even criminal. The husband in *The Pumpkin Eater* persuades his wife into an abortion and sterilisation she does not want because he is in love with another woman. The man in *The Dud Avocado* steals passports, including that of the heroine, who is in love with him, and sells them. Gathered together in a bunch these heroes† would make a good crew for a death ship.

---

* Throughout this piece I shall speak with scant appreciation of writers like Edna O'Brien and Doris Lessing, whose work I have admired, respected and enjoyed for nearly twenty years. In extenuation I can only say that the job of grading and sorting apples probably temporarily precludes appreciation of their quality, variety and flavour. This is not an excuse, but it is an explanation.

† For purposes of convenience the main female protagonists will be referred to as 'heroines', the main male characters as 'heroes'. Any seeming irony, especially in the latter case, must be ignored.

Their books are, after all, about the injuries inflicted by men on women. Since they are by women they are open to the charge that they are one-sided and partisan and such charges have of course been made. Personally I think the demand for neutrality and fair-mindedness in the victim is unrealistic, almost unfair in itself, if the injuries have gone beyond a certain level. It must be remembered that all this was being written at about the same time when writers like James Baldwin were being equally 'one-sided' about what white society had done to the blacks, and being reproved, likewise, for their injudicious tone. Polite society does not like its victims to come and scream in the drawing-room.

However, there they stand, or rather, slouch, these heroes, specialists in every kind of rip-off from the straightforward to the most subtle and refined. Touch them and your child will die (Edna O'Brien, *August Is A Wicked Month*), you will kill yourself (Nell Dunn, *Tear His Head Off His Shoulders*), you will be sterilised and go mad (Penelope Mortimer, *The Pumpkin Eater*), nearly bleed to death (Sylvia Plath, *The Bell Jar*) or get involved in a terrible car accident (Margaret Drabble, *The Waterfall*). These punishments are, fictionally speaking, fairly obvious punishments for illicit sex, a relic, perhaps, of the bad old days when sexual guilt was a good way of protecting girls from having illegitimate babies and ruining their futures. Quite what the present-day mechanism is seems uncertain. Perhaps the connection is more direct – the punishment for sex is not an unwanted baby but the pain and conflict involved in having the actual husbands and lovers about? Only Elaine Dundy has the nerve to resolve her book, romantic novel style, with the last-pages rescue of the heroine by a good man, who is also rich and famous, but as he has barely appeared in the book before, this has the air of an artificial resolution. *The Dud Avocado* is a girlish book, featuring the first of the high-spirited, witty American heroines who come straight down the line from *What Katie Did*. Her descendants transmogrify this into a horrendous irony. The terror of *The Bell Jar* is that it starts on this college girl note. Breathlessly, the girl says:

> We had won a fashion magazine contest by writing essays and stories and poems and fashion blurbs, and as prizes they gave us jobs in New York for a month, expenses paid, and piles and piles of free bonuses, like ballet tickets and passes to fashion shows and hair stylings at a famous expensive salon and chances to meet successful people in the field of our desire and advice about what to do with our particular complexions…

The book ends with the suicide of a friend, following the heroine's own attempted suicide. It ends in the madhouse, the hospital and the graveyard. It is, on one level, every bad joke that has ever been made about the women's novel. And on the other hand it encapsulates so much of the body terrors, the feeling of never going to be ready to inhabit a confusing adult world, which are felt by the prepubescent girl, that it bites very hard, being what so many girls have felt and so few women want to remember.

But the important thing at the time was, and still is, to record the experience, the life of a woman. There was therefore no need for subtle and complex plotting. There is hardly any story telling. A simple linear narrative suffices, for since the books were being written in an almost dreamlike state, between 'I' and 'you' and 'she', and deal with the interior, with reflection and sensation, rather than event, narrative is inappropriate if not impossible. These books are rather as we are when we contemplate our own daily lives, not seeing them from the outside, as plot, but from the inside, as experience. The virtues of the novels, the good ones, stem precisely from this subjective view of the world, necessarily fragmented, as our daily observations are. It is a view, sometimes, of a mind, even at the end of its tether, sometimes of landscape, sometimes of the kind of split observation of what people are saying, and at the same time of their reactions and states of mind, which women, traditionally observers rather than actors, are good at.

From *The Golden Notebook* by Doris Lessing:

> Then there was this moment of knowledge, I understood I'd gone right inside his craziness: he was looking for this wise, kind, all-mother figure, who was also his sexual playmate and sister; and because I had become part of him, this is what I was looking for too, both for myself, because I needed her and wanted to become her. I understood I could no longer separate myself from Saul, and that frightened me more than I have been frightened. For with my intelligence I knew that this man was repeating a pattern over and over again: courting a woman with his intelligence and sympathy, claiming her emotionally: then, when she began to claim in return, running away. And the better this woman was, the sooner he would begin to run. I knew this with my intelligence, and yet I sat there in my dark room, looking at the hazed wet brilliance of the purple London night sky, longing with my whole being for that mythical woman, longing to be her, but for Saul's sake...
>
> I tried to summon up younger, stronger Annas, the schoolgirl in London and the daughter of my father, but I could see these Annas only as apart from me. So I thought of the corner of a field in Africa, I made myself stand on a whitish glitter of sad, with the sun on my face, but I could no longer feel the heat of that sun. I thought of my friend Mr Mathlong, but he, too, was remote. I stood there, trying to reach the consciousness of a hot, yellow sun, trying to summon Mr Mathlong, and suddenly I was not Mr Mathlong at all but the mad Charlie Themba...

I clutched on to the window curtains to stop myself falling and felt the cold slipperiness of the curtains between my fingers like dead flesh and I shut my eyes. My eyes shut, I understood through waves of sickness that I was Anna Wulf, once Anna Freeman, standing at the window of an ugly old flat in London and that behind me on the bed was Saul Green, wandering American. But I don't know how long I was there. I came to myself like coming out of a dream, not knowing what room one is going to wake in.

This fragmented thinking, which nevertheless has one object, the healing of the hero, Saul, this hovering, in a state of attention between dream and reality, might seem disturbing and implausible (I am conscious while writing this, of a line-up of old husbands, friends, brothers, all over six feet tall and saying, 'Rubbish!'), but if these states were so alien and so crazy that no other human being could recognise them, is it likely that the books would stay in print? I think they are new maps – the readers who consult them want to find out where they are. Let us now come to some of the main features of the genre, putting them in bold type. In some cases I shall cite references, in others leave the reader to supply his or her own examples.

For a start, there is:

Unwashed Cups

The unwashed cup, symbolising domestic disorder, is frequent in women's novels and means unhappiness and discontent. In Ursula Holden's novels, for example, states of unhappiness and discontinuity mean rubbish all over the floor and states of content mean domestic order. Letting the rubbish pile up is, after all, a way of saying to the man who shares your life, 'Why should I slave for you?' It is also a sign that you cannot cope. It also means a state of depression where everything is too much trouble.

Another common theme involves:

Unexplained Deaths

I had intended to count the number of deaths in the books I read, but grew weary. Suffice it to say that if the mortality rate in women's novels reflected the real state of affairs, some pointed questions would be asked of the Registrar General on the BBC's *World at One*. Murders are common, suicides even commoner. Mothers die, usually in the middle of many of the books (see 'No Mum') and the cruellest feature of the whole thing is that innocent children, who in these books lead unhappy lives at the best of times, are continually condemned to death (hit by falling masonry, run over or burned to death) purely to punish their parents for what they did. Suicide is more a British phenomenon. Englishwomen usually end it all by cramming down pills. At best, the end of the book finds them touring the graveyard. American women, as befits a pioneer race, normally pick up their packs and go down the road, they know not where.

One reason for all these deaths may be that in books not strongly plotted or having any very clear view of a busy outside world, which is entirely separate from the consciousness of the narrator, sudden deaths and accidents have the purely technical function of hyping up the action and attracting the attention of the reader. This is part of the reason, I have no doubt, but I think there are others. In *The Waterfall* Margaret Drabble writes of the car accident in which the woman, her lover James, and her children are involved, just as the woman finds the man alive: 'It would have been so much simpler if he had been dead: so natural a conclusion, so poetic in its justice.' Later she says: 'There isn't any conclusion. A death would have been the answer, but nobody died. Perhaps I should have killed James in the car, and that would have made a neat, a possible ending.' A feminine ending? At the end of the book comes the same note when the heroine finds that she has a thrombic clot, caused by taking birth control pills. She says: 'The price the modern woman must pay for love. In the past, in old novels, the price of love was death, a price which virtuous women paid in childbirth and the wicked, like Nana, with the pox. Nowadays it is paid in thrombosis or neurosis.' In both cases, although the thesis in the last extract is complicated, I think Margaret Drabble felt the pull of the purely feminine notion of how things ought to go – punishment attends sex – but rationally pulls back, knowing that she will only be using meaningless melodrama. Interestingly enough it is only in the women's novel today that sex is punished like this, although in the nineteenth century the Little Em'ly or Hetty Sorrel theme was common.

It also accorded more with reality – without birth control and with all the social pressures against sin and illegitimacy, girls did kill their babies, throw themselves off bridges and even the most respectable of them could easily die in childbirth. It is an odd sight – all these girls in miniskirts standing on the bridge at midnight crying, 'Farewell cruel world.' Nevertheless, Margaret Drabble, as I shall point out later, is more prepared than many other writers to scrutinise what she is actually saying in her books and make a deliberate attempt to turn away from what she considers weak and feebleminded in the interests of sanity, mental hygiene and the great tradition. This cruel division makes the running critique of herself in *The Waterfall* all the more interesting.

Closely linked with the themes of death and sexual guilt comes the theme of:

Rotten Holidays

Leave home at your peril is what the British women say. And since most women only leave home, it is argued, to have a good time with men they are not married to, the concept of sin, sunshine and sudden death is quite strong. Even an innocent walk round the park will get your dog run over (*The Pumpkin Eater*, Penelope Mortimer). A foreign holiday will get your child run over (*August Is a Wicked Month*, Edna O'Brien). Picnics end in murder (*The Glass Bottle Factory Outing*, Beryl Bainbridge). Unless you are in the house all the time, the message seems to run: something will go very badly wrong. This injunction has been forced on women since the days when it may actually have been true, housework being demanding, families large, and in need of constant watchfulness and TB, the workhouse and the death of the breadwinner actual consequences of inattention to domestic detail. The American heroines, the health and safety of whose families in the old days may have depended on getting into a wagon and setting off to find a better life or going out into the woods to fight Indians, have a more healthy outdoor tradition. Their travels tend to be journeys of self-exploration and although they are not always dream holidays at least they do not, as a matter of routine, end in death.

This state of affairs leads inevitably to:

Unemployment

The two women of *The Golden Notebook* have jobs. One is a blocked writer; the other is a relatively unemployed actress. So they spend most of their time at home, where people come, or do not come, phone or do not phone. Jobs, and especially absorbing jobs, are rare, which perhaps reflects conditions in the outside world. There is, of course, an oddity here, for it is the point at which the author and the author/character differ radically. The character may be a blocked writer; the author is a working writer. She has a job and has either been paid, or expects to be paid for her work.

I am naturally talking about middle-class women. These are, after all, bourgeois novels for the bourgeoisie. The women of these novels are those whose role has, in the past, been as child-bearers and housekeepers and who, unlike working-class women, have not had to work or have direct contact with the world of work. Smaller families, collapsing marriages and easily-run homes have to some extent robbed the middle-class woman of her role inside the home. At the same time work, middle-class work that is, is not so easily come by and idleness, often involuntary, is the result. I think this accounts for much of the sense of worthlessness from which the women in the novels seem to suffer.

Working-class women, even when not at work, have always had a harder job to rear, sustain and hold their families together and they have, moreover, from down on the floors they were scrubbing, from their positions in the weaving shed or from the fields where they were pulling turnips, gained some fairly sound and realistic ideas, albeit in a limited way, about the economic system and where money and power lie. They have known their own importance and they know where they stand.

This state of joblessness leads to:

No Future
By which I mean that in the novels I read I rarely got the impression that the main characters had any real grip on the future – their own or anyone else's. The outside world, as I have said, is not a great force in the novels. The heroines' isolated positions, housebound and out of work, do not give them that foothold in the world which many others have.

Politics and international affairs are commonly seen in terms of a flickering television, a collection of newspaper cuttings, random, barely-understood, totally uninterpreted items. Technically, it is very hard to write a non-future novel, for a massive part of fiction, from *The Odyssey to The Wings of a Dove* depends for its interest partly on keeping the reader in suspense. Where there is no future for the characters there can be no anticipation for the reader, and one of the most useful tools of the novelist in the way of plot instantly evaporates. This intentionlessness in the characters is confusing for the reader because it is partly by people's hopes and plans that we know them. It is disturbing because a lack of interest in the future is generally a problem of the clinically depressed.

Another very common situation is that of having:

No Mum

They usually die. The figure *mother* is super-ego, a conscience, expressing morality for the heroine, either in what she says, or in how she lives. As morality is short in the novels (see 'No Soul') this morality is normally the morality of duty, in much the same form in which it is found in Victorian novels. It is the morality of the 'good woman' who tends her home and family and does not complain. Of course what the death of the mother means is that the voice of conscience is gone. The heroine is out there, on her own. To give a personal example, my own mother protested vigorously about being knocked over in my own, generic novel. 'I suppose that's what everyone wants to do to their parents anyway,' she said in an aggrieved voice. I was furious that she had got the point, but got it wrong, for in retrospect I realised that the careless running down of Mother took place at the point where the heroine had reached such a point of flouting the laws of God and man that she had to eliminate their chief exponent – mother. Sorry, Mum.

At any rate, mother appears to be the only moral authority here. Otherwise there are no guidelines for dealing with the problems with which life abounds.

The women have:

No Soul

'I'm freeing her of me,' says one of Doris Lessing's women, of the child she is abandoning. 'He's such an awful fool, Baba,' says Edna O'Brien's heroine of the husband she is cuckolding. Almost as perfunctory is Frances in Margaret Drabble's *The Realms of Gold*: 'The chief of these elements was Karel's wife. Frances had little idea what his relations with her were, and did not intend to upset herself by inquiring more closely: she resolutely ignored the guilt she sometimes suffered.' These phrases do not come, I should say, as part of long discussions with clergymen, internal monologues or whatever. Give or take a few words, they are the discussion at that time of problems which (I think) cause much more anxious thought and concern in real life.

The truth is that the women appear to have some difficulty in accepting responsibility for their actions, although a kind of generalised guilt is often tolerable, and almost a prerequisite – Margaret Drabble, in *The Realms of Gold* excepted. She copes with guilt by using resolution.

If an air of mild depression hangs about many of the books it may be connected with the general air of helpless irresponsibility when confronted with the facts of life, one of which, worse luck for all of us, is that from time to time we have to admit to our own selfishness and confess that our acts are not of the finest. Here are huge areas of the I-must-have-been-drunk-at-the-time-your-honour kind of thinking; of that mood which says 'this is just a dream' when it is not. But experience tells us that such moods, while common, do not usually cover long periods of time spent packing, contacting lawyers and making complex, secret assignations with lovers.

These actions are complicated and while doing them mundane thoughts will sometimes creep in. 'Will this really work?' 'What the fuck am I doing anyway?' 'Who's going to look after the dog, that's the problem' and even, 'Oh, Christ, look what I've done now.' Born, perhaps, to crush the romantic revival and any other flowering of the human spirit, I nevertheless insist that we all face choices and that sooner or later we have to explain those choices to ourselves and possibly others. In the nature of things our choices may involve cruelty to other people – these heroines cannot admit that because that would mean confessing guilt, which would mean accepting responsibility. And they are, after all, victims, and victims do no wrong, they have it done to them.

In the old days, girls were told what to do by their mothers and fathers until they were handed over to their husbands who told them what to do. This meant that a prime feminine virtue was obedience. But even in the old days writers like Thackeray took it for granted that without a system of cash and protection behind her a girl like Becky Sharp would abandon trust and submissiveness in favour of self-defence and low cunning. Defoe clearly recognised that Moll Flanders, left to manage her own life, would have to take to thieving and prostitution. Both writers deal tolerantly with their heroines, probably because they know them to be living by the same rules as men – trying to achieve security in a world not specifically set up to protect and look after them.

Such women as Anna in *The Golden Notebook* miss out this aspect of freedom – that sometimes you have to be nasty – just as, it seems to me, 'free women' that they are, they miss out a lot of the rights which go with freedom. They know about duty, though. If others need hot dinners, they provide them. If people need psychological help, they will give it. If they themselves need straightening out, they pay a psychiatrist for there is no one to help them. They stay indoors a lot, worrying about others.

Their lives become the equivalent of the long vigils by sickbeds conducted by Victorian women and, like Victorian women, they have all the responsibilities of carrying out domestic tasks and nurturing others, plus the twentieth-century duty to earn their own livings. 'Power without responsibility,' Stanley Baldwin said of newspapers, '– the prerogative of the harlot through the ages.' These women have the opposite: responsibility without power, or at least any feeling of power. Of course they are powerful really. Tarzans, believing themselves to be Janes, they run homes, rear children, earn a living and help others. Small wonder that the men they are involved with, having no function except as lovers, adopt some of the personality traits of gigolos, becoming seedy, faithless and marginally venal. Finally, angry with themselves and with the women, they become punishers extraordinary.

At any rate it is an odd world these heroines inhabit, where rights, duties, responsibilities and freedoms, the acknowledgement of which does, to some extent, hold the world together, are all blurred and indistinct. No longer 'good women' whose duties are all obedience and the care of others, nor 'bad women' of the Becky Sharp kind, nor soiled doves like Marguerite Gauthier, lacking place in the world, function in the world, lacking any real connection with the world, lacking a definition given to them by the world and always believing themselves more powerless than they are, it is not surprising that personal responsibility and decision making are not their strong points.

We might be back in the days before women's suffrage or the Married Women's Property Act. This is a criticism that has often been made. But attitudes move more slowly than legislation and I can only prove this by again referring to personal experience. Only a few years ago I wrote a book in which the heroine, by consistently making the wrong choices, or failing to make any at all, winds up penniless – after gaining a fortune she should not have had – after running over her mother by driving without a licence – living alone in a remote cottage on a Yorkshire moor with her four children, by two different men; a simple, even simplistic, perhaps over-stern moral tale perhaps, but certainly not hard to understand. The book came out and, imagine my surprise, when this decidedly feckless and often wrong-headed person was consistently described as cheery, loveable, spirited if wayward, and the like.

Somehow, I thought, either I or the reviewers had turned this knocker-over of old ladies into Madcap Polly of the Upper Fourth – impulsive, sometimes a muddler but always with the best of motives, and fundamentally a good sport and one of the best. She was in fact being treated as a child. Here and now I challenge anyone to write the same book, but with a man as the central character, and collect similar reviews describing him as a good sort and thoroughly likeable. Harsher terms would be used because he would be expected to behave like a grown-up.

So there we are – no souls, no hopes, no futures – and no wonder the sleeping pills come out. Or, since the spirit of the nineteenth century broods so heavily over us, perhaps it should be the laudanum bottle. But so far I have concentrated on earlier books. Perhaps it is time to look at some recent books written by women and, to alter the perspective a little, not just those of the romantic tradition, but others too.

Last year, for example, Iris Murdoch's seventeenth novel, *Henry and Cato*, was published. She has, very emphatically, never been specifically feminine in approach, has not adopted this author-character stance, nor treated of the interior, fragmented part of the brain. Set very frequently in large houses in London and the country, almost, it seems, out of our own times, the very landscapes seem to distance us and the manoeuvrings of lovers, murderers and friends have sometimes looked like the playing out of some classic game of chess, with moral philosophy springing from addition of a freelance, or 'rogue' piece which can move erratically all over the board. But although in *Henry and Cato* the settings are still the same and the characters still have, intermittently, the air of being moved, by the plot, through a series of moral and philosophical stances by some godlike hand, the shifts of purpose and viewpoint in the men and women of the book as they respond to the action and their own inner workings, was impressive, the fluxes of plot and character were natural and one felt the writer of fiction was here well in charge of the puppeteer.

It can be no coincidence that Iris Murdoch and Muriel Spark, both of whom have a sharp eye for the moral and immoral implications of what goes on in their books, deal in hard edges, construct their work carefully around a strong skeleton of plot and incident, and survey a number of characters from the outside, instead of one person from the inside. It is very much the opposition of the classic to the romantic. Murdoch and Spark invite us to think, while writers like Edna O'Brien invite us to feel.

Self-converted, I think, from romanticism – not surprising, perhaps, in a writer who makes reference so much to the protestant ethic – Margaret Drabble, in *The Realms of Gold* (1975), seems to have made a deliberate effort to bring the author/character heroine out of the victim role and abandon the solipsism which this stance necessarily involves. To do this she adopts, in part, the conventions of the English provincial novel, with its wide canvas of people and places. My suspicion is that it does not quite hang together, as a novel like *Middlemarch* does, perhaps because our society is itself more fragmented than the one George Eliot saw, or perhaps just because the creative elements in artists will not yield past a certain point to force or moral persuasion, so that Miss Drabble, with every good and sensible intention, found herself writing against the grain. In any case, much as one supports the notion of abolishing the masochistic, worked-upon heroine, I am afraid that in *The Realms of Gold* she has been pitched over into sadism. That Frances, the heroine, is a successful archaeologist successfully rearing several happy children on her own can only make us rejoice. That she can witness her lover, Karel, beating up his wife, who has come round to make a scene about the affair, and accept the explanation, as the wife lies unconscious on the floor, that 'She (pointing to Joy) wants to be knocked about. I hate doing it, I really do,' as in any way acceptable (if he hates doing it, why does he?), points to a dangerous mix of cynicism and naivety. Just after this, with the wife still lying on the floor:

> They stood there in the wrecked room, holding hands, contemplating the debris of their own confusions. They were both strong and healthy people, able to take a lot more of the same kind of thing. One blow, one row, was nothing. They would tidy up and begin again.

Nasty one, Karel. Once again, in spite of the trappings, the heroine is none too prone to self-questioning and a bit short on those virtues one might think valuable in even the most successful archaeologist and mother – a degree of charity, a smidgeon of humility. I hate to nag, but the opposite of a Jew does not have to be a Nazi.

In a way, *A Quiet Life* by Beryl Bainbridge (1976) is a saner view of the question. It is also a very good book. Set in wartime, it deals with two children, a brother and a sister, in an unhappy family full of the Puritanism and narrowness of the lower middle classes. The girl falls in love with a German prisoner of war, accepts feeling, accepts the flesh and in doing so rejects the respectabilities, misery and lovelessness of the family. At the beginning, when the brother and sister meet after many years, we see again, in the sister, our old friend the half-mad woman, destroyed by her encounter with freedom in a world where she has no place:

> He was about to order a cup of tea when Madge came into the café, carrying a bunch of flowers. She had an old cloche hat pulled down over her hair. He thought, how changed she is, how old she has become. She's forty and she's wearing a school raincoat.

But Beryl Bainbridge, instead of describing the losing battles of the woman who has rejected her traditional role, goes back to that split in the path which took Madge unwittingly away from it. She shows the even more terrible alternative to getting out – staying and becoming like the others. The message at the end of the book is that the brother, who stayed, has been worse mangled than she is. In a very slight, but powerful book (which I diminish here, I am afraid) Beryl Bainbridge I believe says: *no matter what the cost, it was better; it was worth it.*

Both Fay Weldon's *Remember Me* (1976) and Nell Dunn's *Tear His Head off His Shoulders* (1974) are to some extent reprises of the authors' previous work. Remember Me is very like her brilliant *Down Among the Women*, using the same narrative techniques (in a genre attached as genres tend to be, to the most conventional methods of storytelling, Fay Weldon is an exception), and having the same cast of characters – the clever, lively but stroppy ex-wife, the less-clever but more agreeable, younger and more complaisant new wife, and the weary husband who wants some peace and quiet.

Nell Dunn's book celebrates, as she has done before, the unsinkable qualities of the working-class woman, independent, bloody, unbowed, and without self-pity. But the main character, a woman ruined, still ends up swallowing pills. Both books remind one of the old blues song:

> *Oh there's one in the cornfield and one at the plough –*
> *Ah – (lamentation)*
> *And there's one in the graveyard and one goin' home*
> *Ah –*

For each book deals in the past, and how it became the present, and none postulates a future. These are the novels of Slave Row.

As to *Kinflicks* by Lisa Alther (1976), *Fear of Flying* and *How to Save Your Own Life* by Erica Jong (1974 and 1977), and *Any Minute I Can Split* by Judith Rossner (1972), if their own (late) mothers can tell them apart, I cannot. They form a blur and a blur of horror. Variously described on the book jackets as exuberant, warm, humorous, ironic, hilarious and, separately, on the same jacket (of *Kinflicks*) as outrageously and uproariously funny, these books deal with horrible events like running away from bad husbands when nine months pregnant with twins or running away from bad husbands for bad trips with impotent lovers who are also con-men.

The tales are told in tones of high irony (Judith Rossner is so ironic she can recognise, and deplore, her own ironies, but that does not stop her) with self-mockery and even a kind of jauntiness. After a while one's only comparison becomes that terrible moment when the recently bereaved person is telling black jokes and offering the mourners another drink, and one longs for the moment of tears and grieving which will release the mourners and the bereaved alike. There is a smell of exploitation about these novels which I do not really like, of dance-for-us-Sambo-and-keep-on-grinnin', and a whiff, for me, of prurience, of wanting to read the author's confession about what she really did. Still, in a sense, the clients get cheated. In these outrageous, uninhibited, salty, outspoken romps (I quote again) the absence of sex is marked as the absence of pain, as though anaesthetics had been applied all over the place. You will find, if you want it, more rude reading in *Confessions of a Window Cleaner*, more sensuality in the work of good old-fashioned Colette, and more genuine passion in the work of that celebrated spinster daughter of a nineteenth-century clergyman, Emily Brontë.

Like the real romantic novels, by Netta Muskett, Barbara Cartland, et al, these novels are not about sex. In the hardcore romantic books the heroines want to survive economically and otherwise, through the security of marriage. In the newer versions the women want affection from and real relationships with men, at a time when the old system is changing. The craving is a craving for love and there are ways in which the 'new' woman is far more soft-centred than her romantic novel counterpart who sees, as Jane Austen did, that love, money, marriage and men are inextricably entwined.

As I have been writing this (by now, the reader will not much want to know, with chickenpox), the causes of my depression when, a woman myself, I read so many books about women, by other women, have become plain. It is hard to look in the glass and see yourself covered with spots, but harder still to look in the metaphorical mirror these books hold up to their readers and see yourself reflected back as without autonomy, skills, morality, perpetually wronged and, lacking the weapons or aggression to fight back, barely even understanding what or who is hitting you.

The other image which has come involuntarily and persistently to mind are some passages from the *Autobiography of Miss Jane Pitman*, published in 1971, where she recalls how the plantation owner calls the slaves together at the end of the Civil War and tells them they are free. They can hardly understand. Some go back to work, some wander off aimlessly. She herself decides to start walking north.

I think there is a real comparison between this and the way women see themselves in much of the fiction which they have published about themselves over the past twenty years. Are they, we wonder, without the real felt experience of freedom, or its responsibilities, or the resources to survive, to wander needlessly down to the fields and pick up their hoes, because that is all they know? Or to take the long walk north, without maps or provisions, and get attacked by white renegades who kill them because they cannot stand the sight of their freedom? Or sign up with massa again and be free, but not quite free to the end of their days? Here, I think, is a large part of the question women's novels have been asking for twenty years. And the answer lies in the future, both as it is lived and as it is written about.

***Bananas*, Summer 1977 No. 8**

When this article was published Virago had been around for four years and the Women's Press was about to be launched. On Virago's 2013 website, celebrating its 40th anniversary, there's no mucking around. The very first statement on its 'timescale' interactive feature for 1973 is epic: 'The rise of the Women's Liberation Movement was causing seismic shifts in the march of the world's events; women's creativity and political consciousness was soon to change the face of publishing and literature.'

For my sins perhaps, I was to be quite involved with feminist publishers for many years, being the only male director of the Women's Press for over thirty years but, before I remember those times, I want to trawl back even further to when, as a bookseller, we sold feminist tracts, nearly all having been previously published by American imprints. Apart, of course, from *The Second Sex*, by then a Penguin paperback, and odd volumes by Virginia Woolf and Mary Wollstonecraft, all were sold with no great brouhaha.

Our copies of these and similar texts were displayed in a literary section headed 'Belles Lettres' where resided a strange mixture of old and new titles, mainly thought unclassifiable in a bookshop where subject matter for signing sought to be obvious – 'cookery', 'sport', 'romantic fiction', 'thrillers' and such forth. 'Gender Studies' was not even understood in Grub Street.

The first book I can recall which made a splash came from Victor Gollancz, with a vivid graphic cover: Betty Friedan's *The Feminist Mystique*, published in 1963. Even a year later, when I'd just started work at the Oxford Street shop, the book was kept on the 'New Titles' table, in part as evidence of the then captive clientele of Americans who lived around Marble Arch, near to their embassy and our shop's loyal customers. We had a slight contempt, though of course we never showed to them, when they enquired about what was available which was a 'bestseller'. In Grub Street, such vocabulary was vulgar.

By the time what now is called in Gender Studies 'the second wave' of feminism started I was in charge of buying all the stock for the ground floor general department (as opposed to technical and commercial on the first floor). So I had responsibility for the launch of Germaine Greer's *The Female Eunuch*. It came in October, 1970, already sized for the eventual best-selling paperback it was to become. Smaller than the other hardbacks, in a plain white jacket with bright red lettering, I was gently bullied into taking a hundred copies by the Granada Publishing's salesman on the promise that the author would generate huge publicity.

Granada was one of the trendier publishing conglomerates and though its hardback imprint, Macgibbon & Kee, claimed the imprint for *Eunuch*, it was Granada's Paladin paperback imprint that would, some six months later, launch the edition that eventually sold hundreds of thousands of copies. It took me over a year, until the paperback was actually issued, and against the promise of a window display, to be allowed to return nearly half the unsold original hardbacks.

The same conglomerate was to publish Kate Millett's *Sexual Politics* in 1971, bizarrely under their Rupert Hart Davis hardback imprint with a lurid pink and blue jacket. I say bizarre simply as Grub Street knew Hart Davis as a posh literary imprint. True, the man himself, disillusioned with publishing, had retired to Yorkshire to pursue his cultural correspondence when Granada acquired the company in 1963, but the conglomerate sought to maintain his literary bias, if not his regard for well-crafted product.

It was clear there was money to be made and reputations solidified in the sex and politics war of the 1970s. Germaine Greer was part of the gaggle in *Town Bloody Hall* when Norman Mailer flung 'I'm not going to sit here and listen to you harridans harangue me' at their feminist, screaming faces. But hadn't he asked for trouble perhaps by agreeing to chair the 'dialogue of women's liberation' in 1979, with some of the best-selling women intellectual writers sitting on the platform and in the audience at New York University? It was a running joke with all the publishers' salesmen as they sold me the new feminist tracts that brassieres were being burnt. Angry women were on the march. The new feminist writers were sold as revolutionaries and, as the young Chinese took Chairman Mao's *Little Red Book* to their hearts, so the lady paperback buyers bought all the paperback reprints of Virago to fill their bookshops till their shelves burst.

'Women Writers' became a genre heading alongside 'belles lettres' and 'travel writing' and, where there was a shortage of space, out went the over-privileged dead white males, now a dangerous infection. The likes of Nevil Shute, Hugh Walpole and H. E. Bates were banished. It was time to rediscover lost female voices.

The new feminist publishers never wondered why so many young women ordering stock for what then were called 'paperback sections' in most bookshops joined the revolution so eagerly. It was expected they'd do no less. Certainly at the Women's Press sales conferences it was almost as if the assistants were storm troopers. Those who did not perform as expected of them were described as 'resisting' rather than merely saying no to yet another novel of lesbian struggle in the outback. For though Virago hit upon the rather clever idea of reprinting 'classic' female writers, the WP saw themselves as more involved in the here and gritty now.

But even gold was to be found in the grit. Lady librarians in public libraries across the land rallied to the cause. I will never forget the moment when a local education authority ordered some two dozen copies of *The Lesbian Mother's Handbook* for all their school libraries.

Years before, helping my father at the collection for the *Daily Worker* Fighting Fund held each year, taking place between the political speeches and the entertainment given by visiting 'Soviet Artists' singing 'Cherry Ripe', the only Communist local councillor in the United Kingdom, Councillor Solly Kaye, would wave a postal order for a very small amount and shout: 'Half a crown, comrades, half a crown from a pensioner in Perth...' The glee such news was greeted with rivalled the Women's Press's collective joy as the embattled lady librarians did their bit for the liberation struggle.

Perhaps our feminist press did think itself more earnest, perhaps more 'political' than Virago. We sneered when Arts Council money was wasted, we thought, in the creation of a fancy-shelved Virago shop on a fashionable side-street in Covent Garden. At the inaugural International Feminist Book Fair in 1984, funded by the ever sympathetic Arts

Council and the militant ladies on Ken Livingstone's GLC Woman's Committee, Virago and the Women's Press were careful to show their wares at opposite ends of the Jubilee Hall. The rest of us (I was wearing my Quartet hat) were lined up between them sitting behind our rented green card tables. Whilst the two great imprints looked worthy of stands at the Frankfurt Fair, the remaining publishers looked merely suited out for a village fete.

And it was at Frankfurt when the rancour finally became insurmountable. For a number of years feminist imprints from around the world would meet at Frankfurt to discuss common interests. There was a suggestion, if I remember the gossip afterwards correctly, from the Scandinavians that the imprints request the Fair management let all feminist publishers exhibit together in the same section within the Fair. This was a feature of the International Hall where, for example, all the children's publishers or the religious publishers quite sensibly huddled together. And it failed to happen because Virago and the Women's Press refused to exhibit near to each other. At least, that's what I was told by a group of bemused French feminists, and I've no reason to not believe them. I never dared to ask the Women's Press.

I'd gotten to know the French feminists some years before this kerfuffle when they had sold to an English radical publishing cooperative called Readers and Writers the rights to translate their four feminist children's books. Beautifully illustrated, the stories reversed the fairy stories with girls slaying the big bad wolf and boys crying in the pantry and frightened of walking through the dark forest.

I was a bookseller then, responsible for a large shop opposite Foyle's with three huge glass windows. I agreed that we'd do a window display to celebrate the launch of the new children's series and I painted Winnie the Pooh floating across the window with a balloon, over a slogan which shrieked in vivid red letters as big as possible: 'Winnie the Pooh is a Male Chauvinist Pig. True.'

Within days I had a visit from Methuen's London representative of their children's publishing list ('representatives' was a word Grub Street used for salespeople, which got shortened to 'reps') which then was a division of what sounded like a formidable and mighty concern called Associated Book Publishers. It was the result of the first wave of amalgamating independent English publishers into large conglomerates in an attempt to fight the gobbling-up onslaught from abroad as American and some European publishing giants sought to create the supposed rewards that came from size by buying up the English gentlemen publishers. New management words were abuzz like 'synergy' and 'cross-fertilisation of interests'. ABP, as Winnie the Pooh's original publisher had been synergised into, was then a mighty conglomerate and when the real Christopher Robin had complained about my window display (Christopher Robin was a bookseller in Devon and had seen the window on a trip up to Foyles) to his father's publisher, they felt action had to be taken. We stood our ground, pointing out that the only woman in the Hundred Acre Wood was a rather stupid kangaroo who was consistently side-lined or put upon, and the window ran its course for the two weeks as planned. We sold not a single feminist children's book but our sales of A. A. Milne went ballistic.

These days it seems few lady novelists wish to see themselves labelled by having a feminist imprint publish them, one of the reasons perhaps for Virago to have shrunk and the Women's Press to have ceased publishing. There are still a few feisty small independent feminist presses but, as Doris Lessing remarked, all women writers are always feminists.

Maybe it proves just how right old Lampedusa was when he suggested in *The Leopard* (not that he was that old when he died, in his early sixties, without ever knowing that his rejected and still unpublished novel would eventually conquer the world) of how, in order to change, things must stay the same.

The imposition of a cause's idea of reality on the writer's idea of reality can only mistakenly be called 'reading'.

Philip Roth

When all is said and done, Art is perhaps no more serious than a game of ninepins. Perhaps everything is an immense bluff. I am afraid of that. And when we turn the page we may be very surprised to find that the answer to the riddle is so simple.

Gustave Flaubert

Did feminism change Grub Street? Emma's next saga might suggest not...

THE WRITING OF TARA
Emma Tennant

Cyril Connolly wrote of the impediments and temptations a writer can face when confronting a blank page – famously the pram in the hall, or the 'blue bugloss' of journalism; in my case, a period of enforced ease followed a recent illness. I was too ill to start a new novel but not ill enough to stop work altogether. So it was that I began looking back on my life as a writer and wondering whether there was some half-completed book that might provide an answer.

Turning out cupboards and drawers, I discovered several long-lost novellas and stories – a welter of words that were already fading with age. But it was my partner, Tim, who came across the typescript of my suppressed sequel to *Gone with the Wind*; it had been lying under the sofa bed in his study.

When I sat down to re-read it for the first time in nine years, my first thought was: this isn't as far off the mark as all that – a verdict later substantiated by American writers, Elaine Showalter and Diane Johnson. And my second was: perhaps, just perhaps, the ban on publishing it might be lifted.

It is April 1994 and I am at a tavern near my mother's house in Corfu on a cool, rain-slashed day. The salad and calamari and chips take an age to prepare as we shiver by plate-glass windows overlooking the western coast.

We have two hours to kill before my agent in London calls to tell me whether I have landed the biggest deal in my life.

Much later than expected, the phone rings: I have indeed been chosen by the lawyers for the Margaret Mitchell estate to write the next sequel to *Gone with the Wind*. This delay will be the first of many: either clocks run slower in the South, where the lawyers are based, or decisions of such magnitude must take a great deal of reflection.

Do I really hold in my hands the fates of Rhett Butler, Scarlett O'Hara and Ashley Wilkes? I am already aware that the original novel is the biggest-selling book in the world (twenty-eight million copies) after the Bible. The estate approached the historian Antonia Fraser first, but she turned them down and put my name forward instead.

I made up my mind instantly that I wanted to take on the challenge. But why entrust these mortals to me? I'm not even American and I live in London. Perhaps, in the end, it was because one of the lawyers, Paul Anderson, had enjoyed my continuation to Jane Austen's *Pride and Prejudice* (*Pemberley*). Whatever the reason, I have now been formally invited to set Mitchell's peerless lovers in motion once again.

Now for a few practicalities. It is stressed, in that all-important phone call, that I am not being asked to write a sequel to *Scarlett*, the first approved sequel, by Alexandra Ripley. (This received a critical panning, though it went on to sell eight million copies worldwide.) I need use none of her characters – though I must begin, historically, where she left off. And I am to be a 'Writer for Hire' – whatever that may turn out to be. (By the time I found out, it was too late.)

While Alexandra was on fifteen per cent of the revenue from the book after deduction of commission, I am to receive twenty per cent, as a 'second sequel' is considered likely to glean less money than the first. My agent excitedly calculates that I stand to 'net' $3 million.

Tentatively, my mother and I celebrate as an unseasonable typhoon sweeps across the bay. It crosses my mind that I may be even more unsuitable as author of the follow-up to the most popular novel of the twentieth century than is already suspected by my sceptical friends. But how could I, a writer of slender novels, resist?

Or perhaps, as one friend remarks, I have succumbed to pure greed. After all, with *Gone with the Wind* money in the bank, I could afford to earn nothing and still pay the mortgage.

With supper out of the way, one of the first things I do is to call my friend Hilary Bailey in London. Fortuitously, she is about to embark on one of her historical novels. We discuss how the expectations of readers have changed, and how we can tailor our books to make sense to them. How much modern sensibility, for example, must I bring to bear on a story conceived in the 1930s and set three generations earlier in the American Civil War?

Back in London, our discussions range all through the summer while the Mitchell estate slowly prepares the all-important contract. Why shouldn't Scarlett fall in love again with Ashley, I think – and why wouldn't Ashley show his true colours by letting her down in the most Jamesian way – by marrying a New York heiress? Wouldn't Rhett's manners seem squalid and dated to the reader seeking romance? (Millions of housewives had swooned when the *Gone with the Wind* movie showed Scarlett's coy appreciation of a rape, but that was in 1939.)

My advance, it is decided, will be $100,000, to be paid in quarterly instalments while I work on an outline for the estate. The percentages kick in only after a publisher has agreed to take the book.

The contract finally arrives: it is eighteen A4 pages of dense type. My 'second sequel novel', it says, will belong entirely to the estate. I must obey the rules – which include: 'No incest, no same-sex and no miscegenation' in the new follow-up. I study the enormous document with growing awe, and learn that my manuscript will be locked away forever in a vault at the lawyers' Atlanta office if I fail or disobey.

It is only several years later that I learn of the reaction of Pat Conroy, a Southern writer who had also been approached to write the sequel: he walked out after two years, announcing that negotiations with the Mitchell estate lawyers were tougher than drawing up the Treaty of Versailles.

As the weeks go by, I have discussions with F, a distinguished author and critic, who turns out to be just as fascinated by *Gone with the Wind* as anyone else. He suggests that I look again into the works of Edith Wharton and Henry James, and that I take Scarlett North, after her inevitable split-up with Rhett Butler. I talk to Owen Laster, agent for the Mitchell estate, and he intimates that he likes the idea.

In September 1994, the three lawyers to the estate – Paul Anderson, Hal Clarke and Herbert Elsas – fly to London to meet me. All are in their eighties (and Herbert Elsas is to die less than a year later at the age of eighty-five). They have read my outline and wish to make their comments in person: they also want to see their 'writer-for-hire' for themselves.

Owen Laster, who has come on Concorde from New York, joins us for lunch at the Halcyon Hotel in Holland Park. Sitting in the deserted bar is the playwright Simon Gray, who stares incredulously at my dangly earrings. (How can he know that I'm trying for the Southern belle look?) The meal goes pleasantly enough. Then there's an awkward moment when Mr Elsas leans across the table and says something I can't quite understand: 'Temple...nude...'

I have to rack my brains to remember what I put in my outline – ah yes, he must be referring to the love scene between Ashley and Scarlett in a temple (transported stone by stone from Greece to Newport by Scarlett's millionaire suitor). 'I'll take another look at that,' I promise the trio of lawyers, whose unblinking eyes are fixed on me. I have a sinking feeling that I've somehow strayed into *The Crucible*.

By the time the lawyers have finished their decaff, it's time to talk about the deal. The plan is to market my outline in November to coincide with the global screening of Robert

Halmi's mini-series, *Scarlett*, on television. More money has been spent on advertising this series than has ever been spent in the history of television, they tell me, and it cannot be anything other than the greatest ratings-earner of all time.

After they have gone, I wait anxiously in London, making some changes to the outline. Then I buy the video of *Scarlett*, turn on the TV and sit back.

The mini-series doesn't just flop in my drawing room, it bombs the world over. Owen Laster, who has offered my outline to Warner (the publishers of the first book sequel, *Scarlett*), receives a polite rejection. Suddenly, anything to do with *Gone with the Wind* is right out of fashion. Silence, and an anxious Christmas, ensue.

By January 1995, desperate for some action, I suggest that Laster should approach St Martin's Press (the company that has just published my two continuations of Jane Austen's *Pride and Prejudice*). A couple of weeks later, an offer is on the table: for the US and UK rights, St Martin's are prepared to pay the estate $4.5 million. They accept, and I begin to write.

Spring and summer 1995, I rent a mews house in order to escape the building works next door and gain some peace to work on the manuscript.

In September, I take a holiday in Corfu. The senior lawyer, Paul Anderson, and his wife break off from their Greek Island cruise to come to lunch at my mother's house and I proudly show them the almost completed manuscript of *Tara*.

Paul Anderson chuckles as he sips his glass of retsina. (It may taste of furniture polish but he has perfect Southern manners and would not dream of pointing this out.) 'Last time I read *Gone with the Wind* was in 1936,' he drawls.

The William Morris agency has decided to wait until the manuscript is finished before offering it to foreign publishers. But Heyne, the giant German paperback house, has somehow 'found' a copy of my outline, and offered $1 million; the cat is out of the bag.

Deal follows deal: Japan puts down another $1 million; Italy $330,000. Then there are offers from all of Scandinavia. I am asked to 'talk up' France – which I do, hearing my execrable French ring out in the rented house where I write. When I peruse my copy of the St Martin's contract with the estate, signed only in August, I discover a Book Club deal amounting to $1 million.

A profile of me appears in an 'At Home With…' in the *New York Times*, explaining that, after the critical disaster of Alexandra Ripley's sequel, the estate decided to take on a literary writer; they had chosen me, it said, because of my 'love of narrative.' The first fan letters from the Daughters of the Confederacy and other such organisations began to roll in. 'Remember the South was saved by its women…' I am exhorted, lectured, praised – all before a word of the manuscript has been seen.

All I know as I write is that I'm putting my heart and soul into this book. I talk into the night with Hilary about whether young women today would prefer a 'new man' (Ashley) to a sadistic, arrogant one (Rhett). I study as I write: Marxist histories of the South, analyses of the Civil War and its aftermath, fashions in Paris at the time, Manet's delicious paintings of outdoor balls on the banks of the Seine.

I change the ending several times. And I scrap the idea of taking Scarlett to Scotland, my own home country, and setting her down in the heather to build a new life with Rhett…even I can see there's something a little too purple about *Gone with the Wind* in the heather…

Finally, at Thanksgiving 1995, I deliver the manuscript to St Martin's Press and to Little, Brown UK, whose Managing Director, Philippa Harrison, has offered $775,000 on the strength of the outline.

By December, I am excited and apprehensive. The German publisher comes over for a drink and drops on his knees to kiss my manuscript, which sits thickly on the floor in a box. As his lips touch his $1 million investment, a fax arrives, forwarded by my agent. It is from St Martin's Press. It is clear that the Chairman, Tom McCormack, hates the book. He accuses me of treating *Tara's* prospective audience as 'ridiculous American readers'.

The next day, I'm on the move again. At my new flat, young friends of my daughters are painting the walls. There is no phone as yet, and I clutch my mobile. I have left a message for Philippa Harrison to call me – after that brutal fax from St Martin's, her response will be all-important.

When we finally connect, her voice is strangely distorted – by the paint-stripping, the blaring radio and the voices of the young decorators, two of whom have set up camp in the middle of the floor. But I catch two words which make me spring to my feet, nearly overturning a pot of 'Mango' or 'Fresco', the colours I have chosen for my new, richly-rewarded life.

'It's terrific.' Then, suddenly, the mobile loses its power – showing on the display panel, for some unearthly reason, the words, 'Wow, man.'

Wow indeed, I think. I have already heard that Owen Laster found my script 'highly readable' and that he considers St Martin's to be 'unnecessarily alarmed'. This pronouncement from Little, Brown has to tip the balance. Surely the lawyers for the estate, who have been making friendly noises after their first reading, will be able to persuade St Martin's to see my book with new eyes...

On New Year's Day, by courier, a letter arrives from St Martin's Press. I cannot at first register what they are saying. I read it again and realise that they quite simply dislike every aspect of my book. McCormack complains that I have used the word 'as' too often, and an editor who works with him says, 'It's just not Tara.' They want a new story-line, a list of 'goals' and even a 'whole new sensibility'.

From January to April I struggle to persuade the lawyers in Atlanta that these 'revisions' simply cannot be accomplished.

On 22 March 1996 I am officially fired – by letter. It is not even addressed to me: the St Martin's lawyers have written to the Atlanta estate lawyers. I have failed to set out the desired 'goals' and my manuscript must go into the infamous vault (to join, as I later hear, other blood-soaked casualties).

Letters in my support are sent by the MD of Little, Brown UK, Philippa Harrison, to Paul Anderson in Atlanta. ('The reaction of St Martin's is quite beyond me,' she tells the *Bookseller*). The German publisher writes indignantly to Owen Laster. (Later, Helen Taylor, in her book *Circling Dixie: Contemporary Southern Culture through a Transatlantic Lens*, calls the rejection of my manuscript 'indicative of American hostility towards the British approach to an American and Southern treasure').

Nine years passed. I wrote memoirs, autobiography and a novel, *Felony*, about the crimes and misdemeanours surrounding the writing of *The Aspern Papers* by Henry James.

When I dipped into *Tara* again last year, it was like reading the novel for the first time. There was Scarlett, as maddening and self-obsessed as ever; the ambiguous Ashley; and Rhett – a crook and a sadist who nevertheless carried the sympathy of the reader.

While I was still engrossed in my lost book, a friend brought a Bulgarian writer called Raicho Raichev around to see me. A reader of some of my novels, he told me that he had just printed out an assortment of offers from Amazon. One of these was a full page dedicated to *Tara*, which announced that I was the author, that Little, Brown published the book in September 1997 and that this 'difficult to obtain' volume demanded a wait of four-six weeks for delivery – plus an extra £2 on top of the £15.99 cover price.

At first, Raicho refused to believe me when I said that Tara did not exist – or, rather, that it was buried in a vault and could never be retrieved. He decided to send Amazon a £17.99 cheque for the book.

All this took place before Christmas, and although Raichev's credit card has not been debited, there has been no acknowledgement that the book doesn't exist. Instead, Amazon informed him that the book would be delivered to him 'between 5 and 20 January' – which, of course, it wasn't.

We started to speculate wildly: could there be a *Gone with the Wind* mafia? Perhaps crooks with a stolen manuscript that they photocopy on demand and supply through a fake Amazon outlet? Or is the owner of the clandestine text a nutter who believes that he is Scarlett O'Hara and has a mission to distribute every word written about her?

Meanwhile, I contacted Owen Laster to ask if he could approach the remaining estate lawyers (now in their nineties) and ask them to have *Tara* re-considered. Well, it was worth a try – particularly as there had been no sign of any words from the mysterious 'new writer' who was engaged several years ago to try where I had failed.

And there we have it. Under the terms of my draconian contract, I cannot even tell a friend in any detail what happened next to Rhett and Ashley and Scarlett. My last hope is that Amazon may hold the spare key to the vault: it has now contacted Raicho and told him he must wait a further four-five weeks for delivery of *Tara*.

March 2005

On Grub Street and feminists, it's of interest to recall the creation of one of the leading feminist presses, in the words of its co-founder, Naim Attallah, taken from his memoir. Interestingly, Virago had been created within the Quartet ribcage, until Carmen Callil had removed her imprint shortly after Naim took Quartet over, which is where we start the extract from *Fulfilment & Betrayal*.

With the departure of Virago from the Quartet fold and the emergence of feminism as a serious movement, I felt there was space for a new feminist list that would both reflect one of the most exciting political currents in society and make commercial sense. Early in 1977, William Miller had the vision to suggest that I meet Stephanie Dowrick, who was at the time managing editor of Granada's Triad list of backlist authors. She was a New Zealander, aged twenty-nine, who had been living in Europe for nine years. Before her Triad role, she was managing editor at New English Library, and so had proved her ability to take on huge responsibility. William and his colleague John Boothe had been trying unsuccessfully for a while to persuade her to publish some 'women's interest' titles with Quartet on a consultancy basis. With William's encouragement, I made an approach and at a meeting late one afternoon at my office in Wellington Court found Stephanie matching my enthusiasm for the ideas I was putting forward. As she remembered it many years later, I said, 'We are talking about the wrong thing here' - referring to the possibility of a consultancy with Quartet. 'Have you thought about setting up your own publishing house?'

Having 'arrived curious, but without any real expectations', she said, 'I left with the offer of setting up my own publishing house!' During our meeting, she recollected:

> We talked, summed one another up, laughed and clicked. It wasn't sexual. It was, however, mutual admiration! I have thought about it often and think it is that we are both quick, highly energetic, daring, somewhat impatient (especially you!), passionate and articulate, and, crucially, we were – in London – both outsiders. I am sure I was completely dazzled by this possibility. I know that when I left your office – and I remember walking along the streets outside too elated to get into the tube – I was walking on air. Yet, at the same time, I was almost appalled. (And had I had the slightest idea of how hard it would be to set up and run a publishing house I would have said no. Thank heaven I didn't!)

A week or so later we had another meeting to discuss the framework. I was to take financial responsibility while Stephanie would be in charge of editorial decisions and the day-to-day running of the company. There was to be no outside investment. It was set up with a hundred one-pound shares, with me holding fifty-three per cent and Stephanie the balance of forty-seven per cent. The new company was formed within the Namara Group and given the title of the Women's Press. Its logo was a steam iron, which besides being a play on the word 'press' mocked the repetitive nature of much of women's work and suggested such phrases as 'full steam ahead' or 'don't be oppressed'. To begin with, Stephanie was the only full-time employee and the whole operation was started in her sitting-room in her house in Bow. For a while she continued with her work for Triad and gave the Women's Press her evenings and weekends. Sibyl Grundberg, formerly senior editor at Hart-Davis MacGibbon, joined Stephanie in early 1978, and an aims-and-policy statement was formulated. Stephanie did not see herself as a missionary figure but believed in women working together to take control of their own lives and make their voices heard. The objective of the Women's Press would be to reach a double audience of committed feminists and those non-feminists who wished to read first-class fiction and quality non-fiction across a whole range of subjects, including environment, peace, health, psychoanalysis and social issues. The Press aimed for an initial annual output of about sixteen titles. It eventually grew to be several times that number with an exceptionally active list of perennial sellers. 'Prices,' the early statement added, 'will be as low as financial survival will allow.'

The first titles to appear from the Women's Press were published in February 1978 and had a strong literary flavour. They were Jane Austen's *Love and Freindship* [sic], her early burlesque on romantic fiction from her manuscript notebooks, appearing in paperback for the first time; the first edition in Britain of *The Awakening*, the only novel by the American writer Kate Chopin, a work that had been considered scandalous when it was first published in 1899; Sylvia Townsend Warner's first novel, *Lolly Willowes*, originally published in 1926; the first twentieth-century edition of Elizabeth Barrett Browning's 'verse novel' about the life of a woman writer, Aurora Leigh, with an introduction by Cora Kaplan; and *Lives of Girls and Women*, an important collection of stories by the contemporary Canadian writer, Alice Munro.

That first list was strong, but did not represent the theoretically adventurous books which were to follow. Those more typical books were going to take a little longer to develop and acquire. Coincidentally, at the Cannes Film Festival I happened to see a film called *The End of August*, adapted from Kate Chopin's *The Awakening*. It was a low-budget film produced in America by an independent company seeking a distributor for it in the UK. The standard of acting was high, the story was hauntingly lyrical and the film had been beautifully produced. Although I had little experience in film distribution, I took a chance and acquired the rights, arranging a limited showing throughout Britain. I continue to believe that the story has a magical feel to it on screen and that *The End of August* has a lasting quality.

Feminism represented a new area of publishing at the time, indeed the word 'pioneering' became a vital part of my vocabulary. I was eager to be in the vanguard of this new cultural revolution, one that was far removed from that in Mao's China in the 1960s. The women's liberation movement, as it was then called, was inspiring women to examine their domestic or business lives and have the courage to assert their rights and make their opinions felt right across society. It was part of the unstoppable wave of social change of which the civil rights movement in the United States was a part. Because of its beginnings as a radical movement, however, the public mind saw feminism as being too strident and extreme and under a largely lesbian influence. As time went by, however, it began not so much to mellow as to broaden its concerns and engage women from the mainstream of the population, who were encouraged to join the ranks. By the late 1970s, feminism was attracting increasing interest from all women concerned with issues as varied as equal pay for equal work, maternity and legal rights, and healthcare, as well as education and other forms of what was called 'consciousness raising'. Women addressing issues from a 'women-focused perspective' was still a provocative concept, but women's publishing was to play a key role in developing and refining the arguments.

There was still a long way to go before feminists would be generally accepted as a force for good, seeking reform and justice in matters of sexual discrimination. The media in Britain was not in the main a supporter of feminism. When the advent of the Women's Press was reported as a 'Diary' news item in the *Evening Standard*, for example, the heading given to the piece was 'Yet More Feminism'. 'I woke up this morning,' the writer expressed his reactions, 'feeling that the sun was shining, the daffodils were blooming and goodwill should be dished out to all mankind. But the moment I picked up a hand-out announcing yet another publishing venture, the sun did rather recede a bit.' With 'yet another' he was referring to the fact that Virago had announced their relaunch the previous week.

The launch of the Women's Press nevertheless got a great deal of press coverage, and Hatchards in Piccadilly devoted a whole window display to the first titles. It was a good start and an office was quite quickly set up in Shoreditch High Street, long before London's East End had gained any sort of fashionable status. Stephanie was soon into what would be a five-year spell as managing director, and the Press was fast moving towards the point where they could begin to publish titles they had themselves commissioned. *In Our Own Hands*, a self-help therapy treatise by Lucy Goodison and Sheila Ernst that was part of a widespread movement to share more broadly the insights of therapy – and was a precursor to the 'self-help' movement that dominates so much of publishing today – was the first originated book to be published by the Women's Press. But many others followed. Among the first novels was Michèlle Roberts's *A Piece of the Night*, which came in under the proposed title 'Swimming towards Blue' and was to be a big success both for the Press and the author.

The look of the books was always a passionate consideration for Stephanie and the attention she gave to their design as well as to the editing was an important factor in their success. Suzanne Perkins was the original designer or art director for most of the covers and publicity materials. Stephanie was adamant that the books should look innovative and smart, despite the financial constraints under which she was working because of the strict limits on the Women's Press overdraft. Stephanie and I, perhaps inevitably given the differences in our experience and ideological allegiances, had our ups and downs in our negotiations, but always ended at a position of mutual respect. At one point Stephanie had to fight to defend her editorial independence when I developed misgivings over whether the list was turning out to be too radical. She won her case, but while she preserved editorial autonomy, it was never possible to add to this the financial autonomy she really must have wished for. She also found herself having to field broadsides from the press, and criticism from some feminists who queried how the Women's Press could be a genuine feminist outfit if it was being bankrolled by a man. (Although, to be fair, she worked very hard to make the Press financially self-sufficient.) Later on the columnist Penny Perrick wrote a piece on me in the Standard, headed 'The Man Who Finances Feminism'. It quoted me as comparing the company I ran to a woman, describing it as 'dangerous, unpredictable, attractive'. There were times, too, when I found myself coming under fire from the direction of Shoreditch High Street for publishing material that Stephanie perceived as pandering to male chauvinism. My friendship with Stephanie survived everything.

Notwithstanding all the constrictions it had to work under, the Women's Press went from strength to strength. Generating a widespread debate about pornography, they published two books on this subject simultaneously, one by Susan Griffin and the other by Andrea Dworkin. They were also pioneers in the field of art history, publishing ground-breaking books on women artists and on individual artists, such as Gillian Perry's book, *Paula Mondersohn-Becker*. Eventually the Press also had its crime list, with authors like Marcia Muller and Val McDermid, a science-fiction list under the guidance of Sarah LeFanu, and its teenage Livewire list, which featured titles for young adult women on such topics as teenage pregnancy, vegetarianism and bullying. From the early 1980s there was also the Women's Press Book Club that offered at substantial discounts some of the best of women's writing from across the range of British publishers.

The most spectacular of the Women's Press's commercial successes was Alice Walker's *The Color Purple*, later made into a film by Steven Spielberg. The Women's Press had published Alice Walker's books from the late 1970s, and those of other black woman writers like Toni Cade Bambara, at a time when mainstream British publishing houses were convinced that writing by radical black women could not possibly sell. But over the next two decades there were many other titles that achieved sales figures which would make publishers today feel envious. Among these were Marge Piercy's *Woman on the Edge of Time*, Janet Frame's *An Angel at My Table*, Flannery O'Connor's *A Good Man is Hard to Find*, Elaine Feinstein's *Inheritance* and May Sarton's many books, including her classic, *Journal of Solitude*.

Stephanie left the Press and Britain for a successful writing career in Australia, but several of her books, including the best-selling *Intimacy and Solitude*, were published by the Press in the 1990s. She was followed in the managing director's role first by Ros de Lanerolle and then later by Kathy Gale, each of whom brought their own view of feminism and of publishing to the task. Summing up that early period of truly creative publishing, Stephanie has said what an incredible privilege it was:

> to be able to bring together my professional and political passions in the form of the Women's Press. It was, literally, the opportunity of a lifetime and I was hugely grateful. That it was also complex and sometimes extremely challenging didn't take [away] from the amazing opportunities that it gave me to publish books that I believed were genuinely important and even life-changing, and to get to know and work with some truly exceptional writers. The opportunity honed my intellectual life, my professional skills, and I think it significantly contributed to the person I have become. It demanded a great deal of courage, but it also gave me courage.

It seems to me that one should only read books which bite and sting one. If the book we are reading does not wake us up with a blow to the head. What's the point in reading? ...A book must be the axe which smashes the frozen sea within us.

Franz Kafka

In 1954, the American critic Malcolm Cowley was asked to write an article to celebrate its fortieth year of publication by the liberal magazine, the *New Republic*. He answered the request in a letter which:

> [...] wondered whether you'd be interested in a rather doleful piece, saying that American literature, after a brilliant period, is now more directly threatened than at any time since the Civil War.

As I see it the threat takes four shapes or directions:

1. The general atmosphere of anti-intellectualism, in Washington and throughout the country.
2. The loss of an audience for light hardcover fiction, which was the economic foundation of the publishing industry. (Because there aren't any more 'Captains from Castille'* or 'Black Roses,'† a lot of promising

---

* Cowley misquotes. He's referring to Samuel Shellabarger's 1944 historical epic, *Captain from Castile*, published by the Boston firm of Little, Brown, which ran over twenty hardcover reprints and was made into a blockbuster Hollywood swashbuckler starring Tyrone Power.
† Another error. Cowley means *The Black Rose* by Thomas B. Costain, published by Doubleday in 1945, which sold two million copies in its first years of life. Also filmed with Tyrone Power, it tells the story of Thomas á Becket's father set in the tumultuous world of early medieval England. Interestingly, Costain worked in publishing before his success as a best-selling historical novelist.

first novels don't get published – the publishers can't afford to bring them out.)

3. The tying up of literature with the universities – a phenomenon which, in the long run, makes it less interesting.

4. The biggest threat is the decline of the reading habit, owing partly to TV but chiefly to the collapse of secondary education – high school students aren't learning how to read; they graduate without having read one complete book.

That would make a pretty interesting article, I think. [...]

Our Grub Street had a certain contempt for Yanks with their best-selling phobias and brash, lurid book jackets. Even more for the door-stopping, thousand-page tomes of educational 'readers' issued as textbooks by American publishers with warehouses in Maidenhead rather than trade counters in Theobalds Row. When Pan Books began distributing the Canadian Coles Notes (a guide to passing exams such as A-level English without having to read the set books), Claude Gill sold them from wire spinners in every part of the shop – though we had started with only one. It was demand, and the free spinners, that did the rest. But then our Grub Street could not see that what happened in America would, like the weather, happen here very shortly afterwards.

Cowley was writing in 1954. In Grub Street then Paul Hamlyn's Books for Pleasure were a mere five years old, Penguin were still six years away from standing trial for publishing *Lady Chatterley's Lover* and ten years were to pass till Dick McBride came over from San Francisco and City Lights bookstore to zip up the stock and ambience at its English imitator on Charing Cross Road, Better Books. We did have one great advantage, though, over our American cousins: we still had a vibrant and well-funded Public Library service.

When the sorry tale of our literary decline is finally told, the wilful destruction of the community local library may well be seen as the major contributing factor. You still can get a sense of how glorious so many of our local libraries once were when you pass their now gloomy, redeveloped facades. Take the Carnegie Library in New Cross Road, South London, one of three Carnegies in the vicinity, now all sold for redevelopment by the local council. There once were over six hundred Carnegie library buildings open in this country, all of careful and often beautiful design. As a child, I cycled to Lea Bridge Road in Leyton as the Carnegie branch library there stayed open till eight o'clock on a Thursday night. My parents were not bothered I was out after dark and up to no good, such was the power of the written word, so I could smoke a Woodbine before cycling home with my bundle of books.

The main library in Leytonstone's Church Lane was a spectacular building with sweeping marble staircases, a reading room furnished with huge oak tables and plush red carpets and a fully-fitted lecture theatre, capable of showing films or performing plays. On either side of the grand staircase were glass display cases, lit like department store windows, full of the latest books or selections themed under subjects such as cooking or gardening. There were even armchairs, made of polished oak and green leather, in the library proper where I could sit browsing for as long as I wished. Perhaps Grub Street lurks somewhere still in the mishmash of the World Wide Web but somehow I'd bet good money browsing through a room filled with thousands of bound volumes makes for happier souls than Google Chrome.

Grub Street browsing was an aesthetic – discovering a well-written paragraph which led you into a story or a narrative that hooked you. And Grub Street was always about gossip. Perhaps it's impossible now to know what it was like then, to be the first of the few in the know; to have the story before anyone else; to tell someone, in confidence, knowing they would pass it on to someone else as quickly as you had told them when you had heard it. But you had had the gossip first! You had had the power. Is it possible to ever know that joy again? The new world of tweets has put the boot in. Gossip has been industrialised. Power now is the number of your followers in the Twittersphere, or whatever must-have internet connection will overtake tweets when the young decide on something other to hook up with.

Philip Roth, in an interview with the *New York Times* in March 2014, extended a definition of this new power:

> The power in any society is with those who get to impose the fantasy. It is no longer, as it was for centuries throughout Europe, the church that imposes its fantasy on the populace, nor is it the totalitarian superstate that imposes the fantasy, as it did for twelve years in Nazi Germany and for sixty-nine years in the Soviet Union. Now the fantasy that prevails is the all-consuming, voraciously consumed popular culture, seemingly spawned by, of all things, freedom. The young especially live according to beliefs that are thought up for them by the society's most unthinking people and by the businesses least impeded by innocent ends. Ingeniously as their parents and teachers may attempt to protect the young from being drawn, to their detriment, into the moronic amusement park that is now universal, the preponderance of the power is not with them.

We did think our Grub Street was amusing and we had contempt for the moronic. The powerful for us were the funny or the original.

A sense of this is captured in these vignettes by Emma…

These glimpses of the past were found in a recent house move. They took me back to days long ago and half forgotten. First, I was surprised to find a description of an angry John Osborne visiting my parents' French farmhouse and sounding off about the horrors of England as he did so. What had I done to incur his rage? I had to dig further to find that Osborne was simply angry. Then a charming picture of Decca Mitford comes to light: again, she is scarcely recognisable, but her tone of voice returns to me over the years and I am brought effortlessly back to the Mitford charm (tiresome though it may have been to some).

Italy must have been a powerful draw in those days, as in today, and I find myself lying back on ridiculously comfortable cushions in a house in Porto Ercole. People are laughing and pouring white wine: I must have had enormous fun here and soon I understood why. Rumpole is hosting the occasion and we are up half the night giggling with John Mortimer.

But things can become more serious in my tattered little album – I am lured to lair of the white goddess and see that I have been transported to a world I had never really understood, the world of mythology. I remember suddenly crowds appearing at the gate – Robert Graves, a local resident, is rumoured to have died today and all the world seems to want to know about it.

These vignettes of a vanished past show us amongst others Antonia Fraser, David Hockney and George Melly. I'm happy to see them, but as always, memories can bring sadness. Only George's absolute insistence on fun and gaiety can return us to the happy days.

Summer 1976
The Sphinx's Daughter and David Hockney

A dinner for Violet Wyndham in Elgin Crescent. Long trestle tables, rather off-putting white damask tablecloths – and, as I notice when Violet's friend David Hockney arrives with his entourage, absolutely nothing of interest on the walls. Painters go round looking hopefully – as writers do at bookcases – for something to excite or at least titillate: apart from my Kitaj print of a sagging bum on a background of grey and white cells (if that's what they are) and the caption: 'The desire for lunch is a bourgeois neurotic obsession,' there are only dull watercolours of Kashmir or somewhere (one of these Chatwin, ages ago, thought might be 'interesting', but turned it to look on the back and shook his head disparagingly). So the dinner got off to a rather cool start, and, as with the ill-fated Warhol dinner, the main problem was the proportion of women to men. Celia Birtwell, who is charming and is caparisoned in wonderful, dreamy muslins and silks designed by her and made up in most cases by Ossie Clark, is an essential component of this type of evening. Otherwise, Violet and I were alone of all our sex – and the lights were too bright, causing Hockney's yellow mop to look like a headlight at the far end of the table.

Violet is in her late eighties and moved about five years ago to Notting Hill. She is the daughter of Oscar Wilde's friend and saviour, Ada Leverson, the 'Sphinx', and she is funny and kind. When I go to visit her in the house in Lonsdale Road where she has brought the atmosphere – books, china swans, a sense of warmth and interest in others – from her old home in Trevor Square. I often find Hockney's old boyfriend Peter Schlesinger there: like Hockney, he adores Violet, but of course they can't any more be invited together. I see Violet beaming down the table at the now internationally renowned painter and think of Peter Schlesinger and his handsome boyfriend Eric Boman, a *Vogue* photographer, and of the comfort Violet gave the painter. Diagonally placed behind Violet's house – she lives there with her son Francis Wyndham – is the house in Colville Terrace where Manolo Blahnik lives and where Peter had a room, bicycling back there from Hockney's flat, designed by Tchaik Chassai, which seems to run along all of Powis Terrace. And I wonder, caught in historical ruminations as so often seems to happen to me – what Wilde would have made of my one early Hockney work (stolen in the move to Notting Hill) 'We Two Boys Together Clinging', the pink-lined watercolour was entitled; it was a pair of 'Boys Clings to Cliff all night', the Cliff in question being, so it was said, Cliff Richard. Would Wilde have had a perfect epigram ready? Mostly likely, but I can't think what it would be.

Summer 1977
Mitford Maketh Manners

Meet Decca and Bob in the Hungry Horse in the Fulham Road for supper – always fishcakes, like all expatriates Decca longs for the kipper, fishcake, chunky marmalade, etc., of her distant past.

It hasn't been possible to see them before as Decca makes a kind of royal tour, much disapproved of by her left-wing friends, when she comes over from Calif., as she calls the state where she lives with her American lawyer husband, Bob Treuhaft. The tour consists of Chatsworth; as the Duchess of Devonshire, 'Debo' is famously Decca's sister (the two Fascist Mitfords, Diana and Unity, are either dead or living in France and would not be included even on her trips). Then there's Ireland, where Decca stays with Desmond Guinness, son of Diana and Lord Moyne, at Leiscslip Castle. Bob, like a child brought up on tales of fairyland castles and introduced to them in maturity, seems unsurprised by the aristocratic way of life of English dukes and Irish Guinness's. He would probably be more fazed by the arrangements of the intellectual middle class, of the Bohemians who live in their squats in Notting Hill. 'I know,' Decca says, as she tucks into a large haddock fishcake without any pretensions to culinary delicacy, 'there *is* a way after all of speaking of you and the other Emma.' (Debo's daughter Emma, who has married my younger brother Toby, is Decca's niece.)

'What's that Dec?' asks Bob, as he gazes at the treacle tart and decides to order a portion.

'Emma the Good,' laughs Decca. 'Emma Tennant married to Toby is Emma the Good, while Emma Tennant here is Emma the Bad. Like Louis le Bon – you know, the French kings…'

One thing you can say about Decca is that her voice never tails off. She knows I'm not likely to be pleased at my new nickname and the fact makes her eyes bright and her smile wide. This is mischief-maker Decca all right. I have to try hard to remember all the courageous and wonderful things Decca has done: Civil Rights, her fight against McCarthyism, her exposé of sham and dishonesty in the American funeral service, just to mention a few of them. 'Emma the Bad,' says Decca ruminatively as I force myself to think of the time she went with Maya Angelou – whom I met ten years ago, a true friend – to Arkansas and, posing rather surprisingly as Maya's mother, literally protected her with her body in a town seething with the Klan.

We finish dinner on Mitford stories – the madness of old Lord Redesdale and the impurity of the sisters' governesses, and go out into a deserted street. Bob and Decca are staying in a converted church in Mary Place just north of Elgin Crescent, the home of sculptor Angela Conner and her husband John Bulmer. We share a taxi, and perhaps I'm quieter than usual because Decca suddenly says, as we go down Clarendon Road and turn into the small road, 'Sometimes, you know, I may call you Emma the Good.' But the sobriquet she had first come up with stocks; a week or so on, at a party in Clapham. A total stranger comes up to me and says: 'Can you put me right on this? Are you The Bad or The Good?'

Summer 1978
Damn You England

To Sunday lunch with John and Penny Mortimer at Turville Heath, Tim at the wheel of our old Fiat and neither of us aware we are about to meet John Osborne and his newly-wedded fifth wife, Helen Dawson. A lovely day, roses everywhere – and after what seems only a short drive (though we were held up on the bridge at Henley, memories of dreadful lunches with Old Etonians when my younger brother was at school flooding back) – we're parking by the 'cottage' – in fact a charming old house made famous by Mortimer's story of his father and then of himself in *Clinging to the Wreckage*. We walk in by the wrong path or somehow get lost, and soon we're in view of the swimming pool, recently installed, of which John has been known to remark that to look out of the window on a crisp day and see the steam from the heated pool rise into the air is 'like watching five pound notes go up'. We're both looking forward to lunch. A welcome smell of roasting and basting guides us in via the kitchen. We have no idea, until some minutes after we've kissed and greeted Penny, that the rudest man in England is about to descend on us, bearing, like a primitive type of weapon, a Nebuchadnezzar of champagne. John is with him. The giant's bottle has been well broached.

There are occasions when it would be wiser not to allude to any connection between oneself and a renowned writer, but first, impressions of John Osborne (he has his new wife with him, and a daughter, quiet and, I couldn't help feeling, kept firmly in her place). Osborne, grizzled, exuding spite and dislike of women, stares at me belligerently as we go into the dining-room and take our seats at table. He is clearly searching for ways to be offensive: perhaps it is this instinctive knowledge which leads me to refer to his notorious *Damn You England* letter, written from the South of France and as publicly discussed as a royal decree in the days of Shakespeare. 'Did you know,' I ask, in the most ingenuous tone I can muster, 'that the letter you wrote attacking England was in fact written from my parents' farmhouse in France? Near Valbonne – you had rented it – if that is correct?'

Osborne looks at me across the table like a bull with lowered horns, ready for the attack. I can hear him revving up, and here it comes. 'Dreadful little place. Sanitation bad. Food disgusting.' He eyes me, measuring up further. The Nebuchadnezzar swings from floor to table, froth splashes out, he gurgles and gulps. The Nebuchadnezzar refuses to empty: I see the women looking at the champagne, the playwright's tipple, and seeing the end of Osborne, the dark theatre, the hatred stilled.

Lunch ends, finally, but it's hard to feel like a swim in the new pool and Tim and I announce we have to get back to London sooner than we thought. John and Penny wave us good-bye, and John tells stories of the nightmare Laurence Olivier had been while at Turville Heath filming *A Voyage Round My Father*.

'I think you took it too personally,' a friend says, back in London. 'It's been damn you everyone for ages, with John Osborne.'

What comes back to me as I try to sleep that night is the image of the little house, *La Baumette*, in the hills between Cannes and Antibes which my father had bought before the war, and where my parents loved to go whenever they could. One night, my father found a scorpion in the dark little pantry there. He took a saucepan from the wall and swung out at it – but the saucepan was made of porcelain and shattered into a million fragments, the scorpion scuttling away. I wished I had replied to Osborne at lunch today; I can see him clearly, sitting at the plain little table on the terrace in France under the vine and releasing his Damn you England sting. But I know, somehow, that my counter-attack would have foundered, and smashed into fragments like the china casserole.

Summer 1978
Rumpole in Italy
We found this house in Italy, in the hills above Porto Ercole, advertised modestly – and at a modest price – but when we arrived here it was to find a house like a deserted dwelling in a fairy-tale: a fridge full of delicious, newly-cooked lasagne and risotto, beds made up with clean linen. A visitors' book divulges that Gus McDonald was an entranced renter, the other day; further exploration of study and bookcase shows the little casa to belong to Lord Bernstein. His secretary places the unassuming ads in the national press. How trusting they all must be.

John and Penny Mortimer came today, bringing their five-year-old daughter Emily – and my daughter Rose came with them, also five. We sit on the terrace, or drive down to the little port where smart Romans take houses in the summer months. Or we go across the causeway to Ortebello and do our shopping. Best is the great pine forest we have to walk through, to reach a sandy beach. It adds to the fairy tale dimension, the children running in the shade of the pine trees – then the first glimpse of the sea – then, so much more civilised than a caff on a Dorset beach, the restaurants on wooden stilts above the sand, where Rose and Emily dash in and out of the kitchen calling for the 'cooker lady' and John and Penny and Tim and I drink white wine and eat *spaghetti alle vongole*.

This is one of the most enjoyable holidays I've known – but John, as I note, doesn't seem to believe in holidays: up at five in the morning, he's down at the port with a cognac, a coffee and a croissant by six and when he returns to our little house in the hills he has written an episode of *Rumpole* as well as bringing with him a gleaming fresh fish from the market down there. The easiest way to discover if a person is as liberal as the opinions they profess is to examine their attitude to others after an early start while the rest of the party snores on. John is impeccable in this – not a whiff of moral superiority, no allusion to the morning's stint at all. He does go to bed early, though. And the nights are so beautiful, on the terrace that leads out from the first floor of Casa Bernstein. A tame fox visits it at sunset every day. We sit under stars – more white wine – and talk long after the progenitor of *Rumpole* has gone downstairs to bed.

Autumn 1978
Betrayal

The first night of Harold Pinter's new play, *Betrayal*. There has been so much mud thrown at Harold and at Antonia that it's a relief to see them well and happy – as if the tabloids could actually kill with their venom (and I believe sometimes they can). Every kind of supposition has been made – that Harold can no longer write a play – that the liaison has been destructive to ex-partners and all children, etc., etc. – that it's surprising to find oneself in a perfectly ordinary theatre, watching – with some apprehension of course – a play that is bound to be as far from the ordinary as one can get.

The idea of *Betrayal* – of a love affair running backwards – is brilliant, and it is brilliantly realised. A revolving stage takes us into passion rather than away from it: Penelope Wilton and Daniel Massey are excellent in their portrayal of the husband and wife. But Michael Gambon is best of all, as the wife's lover and literary agent of the husband. This is a fascinating play and the only thing that does occur to me is that it's very funny but no one in the audience laughs. Are people by now overcome by the tittle-tattle about Pinter? Do they wait for 'pauses'? Are they unable to respond, in fact, in a natural way?

I'm thinking all this when loud laughter comes from the back of the stalls. I look back through the darkened audience and see Francis Wyndham there. 'He was the only one,' Antonia says afterwards, 'who saw the point and laughed.'

Mustique, Spring 1979
The Queen's Head

Writing in a log hut where a tropical night has fallen and there is hardly any light at all. The hut is one of three, with Colin's palace of white coral shimmering like a giant meringue on the far side of the manicured turf; later, we'll all assemble on the lawn by his open-fronted temple to himself, and drink vodka and fresh lime. Of course, we'll wait for hours if royalty is involved. I'm grateful to my elder half-brother for giving my daughters – and us – this holiday, but I do find the long dinner parties, even the 'informal' sucking-pig barbecues down at Basil's Bar, a bit of a strain. There's nothing like looking at Patrick Lichfield across a picnic table for hours on end, or being taken up to Paul Channon's house for drinks, to bring on a terminal fatigue. 'How long is it since you've been in one of my houses?' Paul asked on the most recent occasion I was dumped on him. How can I answer? How many houses does he have, for God's sake?

I conclude that these rich, aristocratic guests all cooped up on a Caribbean island one-and-a-half miles long and a mile wide, with its whimsically named 'Lady Anne's Walk' to describe a stretch of scrub and the only hotel, the Cotton House, with its reminder of slavery days in the little gingerbread cottages set round it, are as near as one can get in the modern age to courtiers at Versailles in the last days before the Revolution. There's nothing to do but gossip or watch relationships break up – Virginia, who is daughter of a Woman of the Bedchamber to Her Majesty, described to me this morning a meeting which took place in the privacy of their adjoining Norfolk estate to Sandringham, between her mother and the Queen. 'They sat in the kitchen. The Queen had at least six gins.'

'But I thought she didn't drink?' I said, visualising the solitary glass of wine, as untouched as her handbag is empty, with which one associates the monarch. I'm all too aware of sounding as if I am a part of this world. After having to do the conga down a beach to the sound of a brass band, watched by the Duke of Kent standing stiff as a pole just above the shore-line, brings one more quickly than one would believe to this state of mind.

'Oh, she certainly did when (name of a Royal Duchess) reverted to childhood and demanded a rocking-horse as a present from the Queen. My mother had the Aga blazing that day and the Queen went quite red, pouring down the gin…'

Now it's too dark to write. Is no one expected to want to read a book on this island? The coral palace is lit up, it could be as magical as Xanadu's pleasure dome – but the sight of Prince Rupert Loewenstein, his mind doubtless juggling the Jagger millions, as he crosses the turf, takes the possible analogy away. I fall back to wondering whether the wild-eyed woman, estranged wife of a reluctant peer, who had run down through the trees to Colin's lagoon this morning and grabbed me with an Ancient Mariner tale of broken marriages and new romance, will come to the party tonight. I have to admit I'm glad there's only twenty-four hours to go before we leave. Even my friend and companion Tim, who feels as out of place here as I do – he has had a bad morning, forced by Colin to 'beat' lobsters from their lairs in the shallow, weedy waters of the lagoon – is clearly falling victim to the Court-like atmosphere of Mustique. 'Are the Kents going back to London tonight?' he just asked me through the gloom. We both burst out laughing – as we don't know the Duke and Duchess of Kent (once a year on TV at Wimbledon is enough) – and don't imagine they want to know us. There's only one thing for it – grope one's way over to the mini-fridge and take, like the Queen, a stiff gin.

Summer 1979
The Lair of the White Goddess
We're just outside Deya, in the North-West of Majorca, in a hotel that ought to be wonderful but somehow has a sad, slightly sinister atmosphere, the *Es Moli*. There's a vast pool, mountains tower over us and a small bus takes sea swimmers down to a rocky platform on the coast. Yet – again – there's a putting-off, chilling feel, despite the great heat, which is why Tim and I have come here, to enjoy a holiday with some sun after a Cornish school break where rain and pub were the only features.

Ruth Fainlight, the poet married to Alan Sillitoe, gave us the number of Robert Graves, who famously lives just beyond Deya in the open countryside. We've refrained from getting in touch – for the simple reason, as we discovered the day we arrived here, that the great poet is thought to be dead. Paparazzi line the streets of Deya, the little village where Ruth and Alan long ago lived and joined in the life of Robert Graves. The photographers and journalists push us to one side as we ask if there's any news. No, the poet is dead and they await further developments from the house on the side of the hill.

So for days we've bathed in the pool and in the sea, drunk sangria and read books. Only two days before we leave, I decide – as the rumour was clearly a false one, despite the announcement of the poet's death in the mainland Spanish newspapers – to try to call Beryl Graves and suggest she come here for a drink. She replies at once: friendly, brisk, as if the whole place hadn't been crawling with the vultures of the press, eager for carrion. She invites us over – and of course we are pleased and decide to go.

Robert Graves is sitting outside the rough stone farmhouse when we arrive: luckily, the parked motorbike riders, still waiting for the man who wrote *Good-Bye to All That* to make his last farewell, are invisible from where he sits.

The first thing you notice about Graves is his beauty, despite his great age: another dolmen, like Ted Hughes, I think; and I wonder why these monumental men are ruled, as they are, by the certainty of *The White Goddess* (most of Hughes's beliefs stem from Graves's seminal work on the Greek myths). A young woman – a muse, I must suppose – kneels by the poet's chair, stroking his head. Beryl, the wife, good-natured, accommodating but firm, comes out of the farmhouse and offers us home-made lemonade.

How Greek it is here, is my next thought, as I follow Grave's gaze and look first at his cliff nose, the rugged lines of his face as he stares up at mountains and groves where the god Pan must surely run. Every cliché comes to mind; this is a timeless landscape, the pagan world whose female wellspring the poet unmasked lives here. When – one could almost say if – he ever dies, his spirit will enter an antelope, or a bee chasing wild thyme on the mountainside.

'Many years' – these are Robert Grave's words, as under the new famous large-brimmed black hat, his dark eyes turn to look at me. I understand – while Beryl says she thinks we may all have met years ago – with Stephen Spender and Natasha perhaps – that he refers to the accretion of time, the palimpsest in which he is trapped, the poems and muses and wives and wars he has lived through piled in him like the rough stone walls by the Spanish lanes.

'No, we'd prefer not to come to *Es Moli*,' Beryl is saying to Tim. 'You see, years ago in the Twenties and Thirties it was a small inn with a thriving reputation; then the owner died and at his funeral a stranger appeared and captured the heart of the widow. They married,' says Beryl simply, 'and he was a gambler and a drunkard who raped her two daughters in the dolls' house their father had built for them there. So I've never liked the place,' she adds, and for a while we are all as silent as the poet, while a motorbike rider revs his engine in the lane.

Autumn 1979
Mama Don't Allow No Clarinet-Playing in Here
George Melly and his wife Diana came to Notting Hill – everyone converges here in the end.

I've known them since I was eighteen – George at least. My mother was shocked to hear then that he invited me to his flat and showed me a picture of a woman with a set of genitalia where her face should have been – my first encounter with surrealism and with the paintings of Magritte.

Now I hear their street in North Kensington is known as Muggers' Corner. But I can't imagine George, who looks like a self-made anti-mugging device, either in purple with a great cowboy hat in velvet, or dressed as a rather stout mint humbug in Edwardian black and white stripes, can come to any harm there. And Diana is absolutely unafraid of the possibility of that kind of thing. It is we, perhaps, who have more to fear from Melly; I've heard of his after-dinner act entitled 'Man, Woman and Bulldog', though I've been fortunate enough never to see it; involving nudity and unmentionable contortions, it's a treat which may go down well in Notting Hill.

George is one of the strongest voices against pomposity. I ask him to dinner to meet Bernardo (Diana is away). But it doesn't come off. George and Bertolucci are as far apart as the Po Valley and Liverpool, Novecento and Ronnie Scott's...

Bernardo Bertolucci

Just after the success of *The Last Emperor* – and Bernardo Bertolucci and his wife Clare, a gifted film-maker – come to dinner. Now, after winning nine Oscars, Bertolucci seems to control the world. Armies of men in the Forbidden City; vast tracts of unpeopled land in the Sahara visited for the forthcoming filming of Paul Bowles' masterpiece *The Sheltering Sky*. He talks of tribes found in the deepest South, and his eyes gleam at the pictures he makes unfurl before our eyes. But his real emotion lies in the impossible love between the two main protagonists. 'Keet and Port,' Bernardo says, entering the skin of the self-obsessed pair, desert-crazy, longing for the oblivion of the dunes, 'Keet and Port can't leeve together and they can't leeve apart...' And he laughs, sitting in our first floor kitchen in the house just across the communal gardens from the Lansdowne Road palace his portrait of the fall of the Imperial Throne of China has earned for him.

And gossip and glamour were vital to our Grub Street publishing ways. Naim's personal account of three rather spectacular parties may show why…

The rumour around town in early July 1981 was that Davina Woodhouse would soon be leaving my employment. The assumed reason was not because she was about to marry Earl Alexander of Tunis after a two-year romance but that the publication by Quartet of Nigel Dempster's book on Princess Margaret, *A Life Unfulfilled*, was impending and would put her in an embarrassing position. Her own version for leaving was that she hoped to become a conscientious housewife, though if anyone pressed her on the issue she declined to elaborate. Nigel himself gave the rumour much prominence in his *Daily Mail* diary and insisted that any fears Davina might have about the book upsetting the princess would prove to be quite unfounded. I could understand, however, that Davina might wish to distance herself from the book as a matter of protocol. Her original sponsor when she became a full-time lady-in-waiting to Princess Margaret in 1975 was an old chum of her parents, Lady Elizabeth Cavendish, and if Lady Elizabeth took exception to any aspect of the book it would have put Davina in an awkward position. Her loyalties were all with the princess and she did not wish to find herself in a situation where a conflict of interest might arise. In any case, Davina's leaving was natural enough; it would have happened anyway with her marriage to the earl. Her exit was accomplished with warmth and elegance. Our friendship remained over the years and she and her husband were regular attenders at the parties I continued to throw whenever an opportunity arose.

As for Nigel Dempster's book, there was always bound to be a degree of fall-out. Jonathan Cape, as a publisher in the running to take it on at an earlier stage, had dropped out, presumably not wishing to become entangled in a controversial royal affair.

The launch for *A Life Unfulfilled* took place at the Arts Club in Dover Street. Ritz magazine, which covered the event, hailed it as divine, and according to Ingrid Seward, wall-to-wall hacks were interspersed with blue-blooded young ladies and celebrities could be found everywhere. Personalities who regularly featured in Nigel's column were milling about in force. Peter McKay and Jennifer Sharpe made a big show of friendliness towards the author. In his *Daily Mirror* diary piece, however, McKay claimed the book was heavily slanted in Princess Margaret's favour at the expense of her ex-husband, Lord Snowdon. To place the blame for the breakdown of their marriage on Snowdon for his dalliance with Jackie Rufus-Isaacs in 1968 was to make too easy an assumption. Dempster asserted that the princess's relationship with Roddy Llewellyn did not begin till much later, in 1973. Would Snowdon retaliate on the point, McKay wondered.

Friends believed he might be tempted to set the record straight. In McKay's opinion, that would be unwise, for the Margaret book, though fascinating, was bound to be seen as a whitewash anyway. Intriguingly the book described how the princess was loved for her beauty and wit yet criticised for her widely publicised emotional liaisons, and always found herself in the shadow of her elder sister. But whatever she did attracted attention and caught the public imagination: whether it was her agony over the enforced loss of her first love, Group Captain Peter Townsend, her bohemian adventures in London's glamorous nightclubs in the 1950s, her fairytale wedding to Anthony Armstrong-Jones in Westminster Abbey and the distressing break-up of the marriage, or her sun-drenched holidays on the romantic West Indies island of Mustique. Nigel, the doyen of gossip columnists, explored the background to her eventful life and the reasons for its turbulence.

Reviews for the book were mixed but that did not stop it being a bestseller. Some people took exception to my having published it, and one particular criticism came from a wholly unexpected source. Victoria Asprey, John's wife [Naim was at this time joint managing director of Asprey's, the royal jewellers], whose mother was married to the owner of the Léoville Barton vineyard, objected fiercely to a passage that named Barton's nephew as having had an amorous episode with the princess. Victoria telephoned me, incensed that I should be publishing a book she described as scurrilous, especially when her husband and I were such close associates, and asked for it to be withdrawn instantly. Her reaction was astonishing and I became angry at this unwarranted interference that she knew perfectly well was out of order. I stood my ground resolutely and our conversation came to a sudden close. Victoria and I did not speak for nearly a year after that. In the end it was John's intervention as peace-maker that restored polite relations.

At the time, most of the British press looked on me in a favourable light. They admired my enthusiasm, not to mention my recklessness. I made news by acting on impulse and occasionally disregarding financial risks if I felt it was in the artistic or public interest to see something published. Headlines in the Tatler's 'Bystander' column encapsulated the prevailing response to me by pointing out that: 'with oil millionaire Algy Cluff buying up the *Spectator* and *Quarto* [later to be amalgamated with the *Literary Review*] and wealthy Arab Naim Attallah supporting Quartet Books and the Literary Review, who needs the Arts Council?' The article went on to announce that one of Quartet's offshoots, Robin Clark, was to publish three first novels in paperback: Sally Emerson's *Second Sight*, Julian Barnes's *Metroland* and Dee

Phillips's *No, Not I. Second Sight* won a *Yorkshire Post* prize for best first work and Julian Barnes landed the Somerset Maugham Award.

I was still very much in a hurry to make our presence felt wherever it mattered most. The cultural future of an advanced nation lies in its emerging talent. For this reason Quartet sought to concentrate on the discovery of new writers rather than the exclusive pursuit of established names. We took chances on relatively unknown authors and worked hard to promote their work. Sometimes we failed through misjudging the prevailing mood or because we were ahead of our time. There were instances where we even lacked the essential resources but did not let that stop us. We improvised and published books that ultimately had to be remaindered despite their excellence, simply because the reading public was not yet ready to accept the subject or the concept. Sadly, this often happens in the publishing world. Books are similar to paintings in that they may be rejected initially only to be recognised as masterpieces after their creators are long dead.

…Rebecca Fraser, the daughter of Lady Antonia…was among the first of a new breed of young women who would inhabit the offices of Quartet and enhance the literary buzz, extending the company's reach to take in a social circle it had not properly targeted before. The general perception was that we were a left-wing imprint. We needed to shed this restrictive image, considering ourselves to be much more than it implied. Besides being critics of the Establishment, we also had to penetrate its protective walls. The reputation we were beginning to forge was of a publisher not labelled in any way but drawing its material from every sector of society. Quartet was on the road to becoming an imprint for its time and we relished the plaudits that would come its way in the following years.

*

November 1981 had seen the publication of *By Invitation Only*, a softcover book in which Richard Young's lens and Christopher Wilson's pen recorded the famous, the glamorous, the ambitious, the tasteless and the shallow as they socially revered, engineered and mountaineered their way amid the party set of the day. In its pages could be found the chic and cheerful of café society hard at their occupation. The tools of their trade were a champagne glass and a black bow tie; their place of work could be anywhere within the gilded environs of Mayfair. Their only task was to have fun; their only ambition was to come by as many different pasteboard passports to pleasure as possible – each one engraved 'By invitation only'.

Peter Langan, the infamous owner of Langan's Restaurant in Stratton Street, wrote in his foreword to the book, which he had scribbled on the back of David Hockney's menu:

> God alone knows why I should introduce you to this book. The people in it veer between the awesome and the awful. Wilson and Young who wrote it and took the pictures are the only two people who can grease their way through a door without opening it. Café society will suffer as a result of its publication. They'll all buy it, and they'll all condemn it. They'll also want to take a quick peek at the index to see whether they're in it. I don't want discarded copies cluttering up my restaurant after they've finished reading it for the 297th time, so I beg you to take it home with you, put it out on your coffee table, and remind yourselves not to be so silly as to want to take part in the high life. They're a lovely lot but sometimes they give you the skids, you know.

The cover of the book featured a dazed-looking Lord Montagu clutching a glass with both hands and a cigar between his fingers. The inside cover flap stated that such is the paradox of café society that many of its components who appear in these pages would, on the whole, prefer to be absent. Many others who have been excluded would prefer to be included. It must be made clear that some of the more arcane practices described herein apply to the latter grouping and not the former.

The illustration on the back cover showed Peter Langan in a total state of inebriation face down on the floor of his own restaurant. Appropriately enough it was at the restaurant that the book launch was held. On the night, a party for two hundred and fifty people turned into a bash for five hundred of London's most diligent freeloaders, or so reported the *Daily Mail*, which then went on to say:

> Naim Attallah's penchant for bacchanalia was put sorely to the test. He played host to the cream of Nescafé society which featured in the tome. But the cast was studded with faces who did not possess the necessary encrusted invitation card. At one point the crush was so great the PR man Peter Stiles felt it necessary to elbow his way out of a corner where he was trapped by columnist John Rendall and his PR wife Liz Brewer. Alex Macmillan the publishing mogul and grandson of Harold Macmillan and Prince Charles's personal valet Stephen Barry made sure they were adjacent to the food, whereas Gary Glitter and Bryan Ferry stuck to the wine on offer.

The book sold extremely well. It was predictably considered scandalous by some, entertainingly outrageous by others, and people outside café society did not give a jot about it either way. I came in for some personal admonishment from certain close friends who thought I should have imposed a more selective policy on who actually got into the book; there were faces whose presence in its pages could cause great embarrassment and even grief to others. They failed to understand how for me, as a publisher, any form of censorship would have gone against the grain.

In stark contrast with the buoyant market Quartet tapped into for *By Invitation Only*, a book in the same format that we confidently expected to justify a print-run of a hundred thousand copies bombed, with final sales figures of only nine thousand. This was *Settling Down*, the book on Prince Charles by James Whitaker. The mystery of its demise, reported *Tatler*, had caused its publisher 'to work overtime on his worry beads'. It was true enough. To have the title fail so dramatically after Quartet's publicity machine had been relentless in its promotion was for me a serious blow. While some royal observers considered it the best book of its kind that year, the public at large turned its back on it for no apparent reason. It simply would not move out of the warehouse. We kept asking ourselves what went wrong, but were unable to find a satisfactory answer.

Whitaker himself blamed Quartet for the failure, but without producing any evidence to support his contention. The impression he made on me was that he considered himself God's gift to the royal family – an attitude that did not endear him to the public, to whom it came across as pure arrogance. Matters were not helped either when he appeared on *Nationwide* [an early evening BBC chat show/news programme] dressed in his wildfowling kit, complete with night-view binoculars. It must have been one of the most unappealing television moments ever. At least Whitaker had the grace to concede that his style was maybe a bit racy for the shires.

One of the things I love about publishing is its unpredictability. You can seldom gauge the mood of the nation when it comes to books. Either you are too late with a trend, or you are ahead of your time; or you happen to choose a subject that turns out to appeal to very few people, of whom you may be one. This very aspect of publishing brings with it exhilarating rewards, so in the end who cares? Long hours of stress may be banished by a single stroke of good fortune, and we all live in anticipation of that happening to us now and then.

*

On 28 February 1984 we celebrated the publication of Derek Jarman's autobiography *Dancing Ledge* by throwing an outrageous party at the Diorama in Regent's Park. All a guest needed to do to gain entry was buy a copy of the paperback edition of the book for a cut price of five pounds. A large proportion of London's gay community converged on the venue in a state of high anticipation and were admitted so long as they were clutching a copy. The numbers who gained access rose dramatically till they reached a figure later estimated at twelve hundred. The crush became so intense that there were fears for public safety and damage to the very fabric of the building. It was far from being an exclusively gay affair. The crowd was made up of a heterogeneous mix of literati, aristocrats, Sloane Rangers, showbiz personalities and punks. Collectively they represented the most colourful of London's hedonistic high-camp society, as well as its most illustrious. All the beautiful people stood side by side with the ugly, the profane and the bizarre, and were letting their hair down without the least regard for propriety or convention.

The all-night event turned into an orgy of excess resembling a saturnalia. Into the midst of this phantasmagoric confusion and merriment there erupted a surprise cabaret organised by Derek Jarman, the star of which was Elisabeth Welch, the sultry-voiced singer who, at seventy-six years old, was a veteran of numerous musicals and for many a living icon. Escorting Miss Welch was a troupe of fire-eaters who set off total panic among the crowd. The observer who best summed it all up was Auberon Waugh in a piece in *Private Eye*, written in his

132

uncannily insightful style and accompanied by a cartoon by Willie Rushton (the original of which still hangs in my office today):

> Latest entertainment idea to hit the London scene is a group of hideous naked women and one man called the New Naturalists. I saw them at a party given by Naim Attallah the Lebanese [sic] philanthropist, but now they are everywhere. They come on stage completely naked except for combat boots, their bodies painted in green and blue. Also painted blue is what could be described as the man's generative organ, but might more accurately be called his willie.

> They start peeing all over the stage and everybody shrieks with laughter. Those who stayed on at the Quartet party – for a sensitive autobiography called *Dancing Ledge* by 1960s raver Derek Jarman – had the enjoyable experience of seeing it all cleared up by Miss Bridget Heathcoat-Amory, one of the most enduringly beautiful of Naim's string of delicious debs. I wonder if the Church of England should consider a Thanksgiving Celebration Service of Relief along these lines.

The party was widely covered by the press, with pictures of the Marquess of Worcester with Lady Cosima Fry, Aileen Plunkett with her grand-daughter Marcia Leveson-Gower, and Viscount Althorp, now Lord Spencer, brandishing cash in hand to acquire his passport to entry.

Dancing Ledge was Derek Jarman's first major work of autobiography. He was already established as Britain's most controversial independent film-maker and the book gave a kaleidoscopic account of his life and art up till then, from sexual awakening in post-war rural England to the libidinous excesses of the Sixties and subsequently. He told his story with openness and flair, describing the workings of the imagination that lay behind the making of the films *Sebastiane, Jubilee* and *The Tempest* and the frustrations he was suffering over his as yet unrealised project, *Caravaggio*. This was to be made in 1986 with Nigel Terry, Sean Bean and Tilda Swinton, the same year in which he discovered he was HIV positive.

Dancing Ledge was republished by Quartet in 1991 in response to public demand. Working in the shadow of his diagnosis, Derek Jarman managed to fulfil himself as a unique creative spirit, with an extraordinarily productive output in various fields, in the few years he had left. He was a prophet of punk who linked homoerotic imagery and thought with increasingly profound themes of time and death. More films were produced and he painted and wrote poetry. He died from the effects of AIDS on 19 February 1994 at his Prospect Cottage on the shingle banks at Dungeness in Kent, where he created an extraordinary garden in his closing years. It mixed indigenous maritime plants with stones from the beach and sculptural *objets trouvés* washed in by the sea, and it makes a strangely haunting and touching memorial.

The extracts here from Naim's memoirs go way back, nearly thirty-five years ago, describing a book, an author and a Frankfurt Book Fair where attitudes and behaviour then seem inconceivable now. The extract commences with a description of a coffee-table 'art' book of mainly colour photographs, whose author instigated the ensuing dramas...

The book... *Tattoo* by Stefan Richter, who had travelled extensively to gather his material. Initially his enterprise aroused suspicion from the artists and their models, but Richter had been able to forge friendships with many of them and gain their confidence. They came from a wide cross-section of society, and were 'normal' in every respect except for their admiration for an ancient art form from the Far East that the West had chosen to relegate to a symbol of decadence. Richter's aim was to restore the tattoo to its rightful status as a visual embellishment of high quality and by so doing reassert the credibility of those who wore them and rescue them from the stigma of freak-show connotations. Many fascinating details emerged about the art and the painstaking perfectionism which always surrounded its creation. Tattoo attested to the imaginative brilliance of a select group of artist designers who made the human body their canvas. Yet, as well as beauty and intricacy, some of the designs could also reflect deeply disturbing undercurrents, especially when they touched on the bizarre, the occult and the primitive. Then the beauty could be perverted into something so weird that it shocked the senses. There were those who chose to have their entire bodies tattooed from top to toe so that no area of natural flesh remained and even their genitals became hardly distinguishable. For some of them this was a devastatingly flagrant gesture of sheer exhibitionism but the motives of others were perhaps more disturbing.

The book was costly to produce and a great gamble. Some might have found it offensive, representing a desecration of the human body. Others, while appreciating its art, might have found it most unsettling or simply too peculiar. The potential audience for it was an unknown quality and those to whom it could be expected to appeal directly were not likely to be among the ordinary reading public. It was hard to see, either, where it would fit in with traditional press expectations. As it happened, the book's cultish status was to save the day. While it did not become a bestseller, neither was it a failure. The experiment was worth the effort and helped to reinforce the view that Quartet's vision was infinitely enterprising. There were, however, to be consequences I could never have foreseen and which I did not link at first with *Tattoo*.

Every year, when attending the Frankfurt Book Fair, I stayed at the celebrated Nassauer Hof Hotel at Wiesbaden, where I was exceptionally well treated and had a magnificent suite allocated to me. On one of these trips, several years after the publication of *Tattoo*, I ran into problems at Heathrow, before I had even left England, when I found my flight reservations had been cancelled for no apparent reason. I then had a most difficult time securing an alternative flight, but managed it in the end. On arrival at the Nassauer Hof I found an embarrassed staff at reception who were perplexed to see me. Only two days before, they said, my secretary had phoned to cancel my reservation. I assured them that this was not the case. Alas, the hotel was now full to capacity. The reception manager spent a long time on the telephone to try to find me acceptable accommodation, and in the end he secured a suite for me at a nearby hotel that was on a par with my usual accommodation. I checked in at the new hotel with a great sense of relief and a growing suspicion as to who the perpetrator might be.

Despite the good sales we had achieved for *Tattoo*, a dispute had arisen with Stefan Richter over the royalty applicable to five hundred copies which he had himself sold at a fifty-per-cent discount. Quartet maintained that, according to the terms of the contract, the royalties should be calculated on the price received, whereas Richter insisted they should be levied on the full cover price. I held my ground and refused to budge. Richter then became abusive over the telephone, but I would have none of it. He took to haranguing David Elliott on a regular basis, threatening to use less conventional methods, including force if necessary, to get what he saw as his due. I would not be intimidated and told David to take no notice of these ravings. In his last conversation with David, Richter hinted that strong-arm tactics would now be put in motion and I would live to regret my obstinacy.

Richter was a manic personality who, because of his particular interest, frequented a milieu in which psychedelia was the prevailing style and exponents subverted the art of the tattoo by representing visions of the Gothic or the visually provocative, including explicit sexual postures. The sinister shadow of this world fell on the book fair and the question became to what lengths would the disgruntled author be prepared to go? We were soon to find out when David Elliott and I arrived at our stand in the International Hall to be greeted by a pungent smell so nauseating that we had to flee before it overcame us. We alerted security, who quickly confirmed that a powerful chemical compound had been left exposed at the back of the stand, and some of it had been sprayed on the carpet to make sure of its overwhelming effect. The odour was so vile that we could not venture into the vicinity for several hours while the work of removing the residue and thoroughly washing the carpet went ahead. Simultaneously it emerged that pornographic leaflets, showing myself at the centre of an orgy with various naked females – one of them giving me a blow-job while the others ravaged different parts of my body – had been left on every British publisher's stand alongside an obscene poem.

Whenever the Frankfurt Book Fair was on, Richter used to come to it almost every day with his heavily made-up English wife, both of them dressed outlandishly. Her customary gear was a tight black-leather outfit, sometimes with body-hugging trousers to create a highly erotic effect, and a pair of exceptionally elevated high-heeled shoes. She looked like the living subject of an Allen Jones painting. His outfit was in a similar vein, though without the high-heeled shoes, and as an equivalent to her make-up, he usually wore some weird punkish ornaments to signal his bohemian proclivities. We felt sure a visitation from him must be imminent and reported the matter to the police. They showed very little interest in the affair, even though we emphasised he was capable of extreme recklessness and was perhaps bold enough to inflict some physical harm. Reluctantly they agreed to question him if he should show up and went away with our full description. Sure enough, as we had anticipated, he was unable to resist the temptation of coming to the fair to survey the havoc his actions had caused. As always he arrived with his wife in tow. She was instantly recognised from her bizarre get-up and apprehended on the spot. Richter was not far away and was similarly stopped. With a disarming smile, he denied all knowledge of anything that had happened and accused us of waging a war of attrition against him for having demanded his proper rights. The police took the matter no further and he was set loose to roam the fair in a defiant mood.

I never stayed the full course at Frankfurt but always returned to London after four nights to get on with other tasks. News of my mishaps had preceded me and Andrew Moncur of the *Guardian* was already at work preparing a diary piece declaring how the Frankfurt Book Fair had 'turned out to be a real stinker – perfectly foul – for Naim Attallah' and trying to account for 'the sheer, ripsnorting campaign of sabotage'. The only thing to be auctioned at Frankfurt, according to one publisher, had been copies of the defamatory leaflet, while the tale of the 'foul stench' had grown in the telling to where it included 'buckets of ordure being dumped around'. 'Who could possibly do these things?' asked Mr Moncur. 'If Quartet has suspicions, it isn't saying.' All he could think of was a dispute with the Women's Press in 1991 that had led to staff changes and angered some of their published authors, though it was inconceivable 'that the faintest trace of suspicion should fall there'.

Meanwhile David had been left holding the fort at Frankfurt prior to its close. As soon as I was out of the way, Richter approached him for a chat in a less bellicose frame of mind. He was still reeling, he said, from our refusal to pay him the full amount of royalties according to his interpretation of the agreement and would be instituting legal proceedings against us in London. Nonetheless Richter managed to sweet-talk David, who was now leaning more towards finding a way to resolve the dispute amicably. The line David took was that *Tattoo*, having been the moderate success it was, could never justify a legal battle that would be to no one's benefit. Leaving principles aside, a sensible approach might save both parties from a mutually damaging confrontation. He told me that, underneath it all, Richter had a soft spot for us both and would love to close the matter on a happy note.

I decided to heed David's advice and paid Richter the additional royalties he was claiming. The following year at Frankfurt he visited the Quartet stand regularly and inscribed a copy of his latest book to me (not published by us) with some warm words that helped to make up for the bad things he had been saying about me twelve months earlier...

The Frankfurt Book Fair of 1987 was an eventful one for us, with the appearance of *Women* [Naim's first book, published in 1987] looming large against a background of the already described incidents concerning Mr Richter and his book *Tattoo*. As the whole book trade knows, the fair takes place early in October each year, when publishers from across the world converge on the city to exhibit their books and acquire and sell manuscripts. It is a kind of jamboree where publishers shed their inhibitions once a year and behave as if it were one enormous office Christmas party, similar in format but on a far larger scale. The liberals, those with high ideals, mingle with their more sedate and conservative counterparts; the pious and the profane go arm in arm; pornography to suit all tastes displays for the initiated its explicit art, which has flourished since the advent of civilisation. The book fair in itself is a great arena of learning. No taboos exist except in the minds of a negligible minority and nothing is forbidden so long as it sells. Presentation and the ability to deal with any subject under the sun are what matter most, along with the conceptual arguments and ambiguous phrases that are a publisher's stock-in-trade and induce a belief in a magic art that only publishers are privy to.

In the airless and sometimes stifling atmosphere of the vast main hall, the sense of competition rises to a crescendo as the big fish of publishing attempt to outdo each other, showing off their financial muscle to gain the ascendancy in the bidding wars. In the midst of all this the small publisher hardly has a toehold. He is a minnow among the leviathans and can only watch in awe and wish he could rank alongside them. Yet no publisher worth his salt can afford to stay away. Ideas are formulated, concepts take shape and random encounters often lead to worthwhile acquisitions.

My first visit to Frankfurt had been in 1976 when I was completely new to publishing. I was a tyro in a world where most things were strange to me. I had to keep my wits about me and take in as much as I could. At the same time, I had to pretend I had more insight into the arcane business of publishing than I actually possessed. Any display of ignorance or naivety would have worked to my disadvantage, making fair game of me as an inexperienced newcomer. Hardened publishers are a breed apart. They are very protective of their own areas of expertise and are seldom generous in paying tribute to competitors. They do not embrace change easily, nor do they welcome strangers into their midst with open arms. Their view of their own profession is somewhat elitist, and they close ranks to shun those whom they consider to be parvenus – not for the reason that they lack ability, but simply because they do not possess the right credentials. Well, I thought, I was now one of them whether they liked it or not, and I was certainly not for turning.

That book fair of 1976 was memorable for me for many reasons. It gave me the chance to get to know William Miller and John Boothe better. They were there with Brian Thompson [Miller, Boothe and Thompson were three of the original founders of Quartet. Thompson would leave soon after this fair] and our newly recruited sales director, David Elliott, who was still working out his notice with Words & Music. David was due to join us that December, but meanwhile he was spending a great deal of time with us and he bonded with the group from the start. Another major reason for the memorable nature of that Frankfurt was that I suddenly became aware of the distance I had to travel before becoming a publisher of note. Enthusiasm and determination I had in abundance, but there was no short cut I could take to avoid the blood, sweat, toil and tears.

Subsequently the book fair became an annual ritual I kept up religiously, despite the increase in my other commitments. For more than two decades, the first two weeks in October were reserved for what I called intellectual pursuits and the chance to fraternise with booksellers from all over the world. The change of scenery, and one's immersion in every aspect of the written word, confirmed one's belief in the fellowship of the pen. The multitude of people, merchants of their own languages, of different races and creeds, packing the large complex of exhibition halls, proved at the very least that words are still the currency of communication and a potent force for both good and evil.

The lighter and brighter side of the Frankfurt Book Fair was the opportunity it gave me to get to know the Quartet staff in a more personal way, in a different environment and at a more leisurely pace than was usually possible. Formalities were dispensed with and a camaraderie of equals developed naturally. Whereas in London I was far too occupied to develop that sort of relationship, at Frankfurt it simply happened. My mode of operation in London focused on my immediate circle of young ladies, with whom I communicated frequently, dispensing with formalities in favour of a more relaxed atmosphere. They handled the most sensitive information and had the advantage of free access to me at all times. Their close proximity became an integral part of the merry-go-round that made Quartet not only a formidable force in publishing terms, but also a place of learning where fun was intrinsic to its culture.

Quartet became a finishing school, not of manners and graces, but of self-discovery and how best to bring out a latent talent with the right encouragement. There was no inculcation. It was a gradual evolution that brought with it an unshakeable self-assurance. We operated to the envy and consternation of others. Some found us impossible to understand; a few wondered how we ticked and what drove us forward; the rest were simply baffled. However, incessant speculation kept us in the public eye to such a degree that promotional advertising began to become superfluous. We were getting it all for free. *Private Eye* naturally extended its coverage to Frankfurt. A typical 'Grovel' piece ran as follows:

> I hear that gorgeous pouting Selina Blow has been selected from his harem to accompany Naim Attullah-Disgusting to this year's Frankfurt Book Fair [1987]. The vivacious Ms Blow tells me that she is required to get into training for the fair by playing ping-pong with the Ayatollah in the basement of his luxury Poland Street HQ. The pair has been entered for the Ugandan mixed doubles event, I understand.

It was customary for me to take a young lady to Frankfurt to act as my assistant during the four days I spent there. This had nothing to do with the contingent from Quartet who manned our stand. My visit, though part of Quartet's presence, was independently planned so as to leave me the maximum flexibility. My assistant stayed with me at the Nassauer Hof, Wiesbaden, while the people from Quartet were booked in at different locations in the same town. Each party retained its autonomy, but we all dined together in the evenings to debrief and review the day's happenings.

L ike most of Grub Street would do, Frankfurt changed over the years. The increasing power of literary agents is just one example. My early Frankfurt fairs saw the odd agent's stand, some even sharing with publishers to offset the expense. And since the point of attending an international gathering was to meet foreigners, the idea of making appointments with London-based operations seemed an absurdity. Bumping into them at the hotel bars or walking through the aisles was another matter, though few agents could or would match the expense accounts of the conglomerates.

But as the remainder merchants began to encroach into the main exhibition halls as the costs of Frankfurt rose and the empty stands needed filling, so the idea of an Agents' space took hold. When the London Book Fair brazenly created a separate area with its own security perimeter, Frankfurt fought back bigger and better. Not only did you need an appointment to enter the 'International Agents Centre', your bags were searched and a paper form with a plastic cover was pinned over your Frankfurt credentials and if there was no trace of the appointment, the receptionist would telephone ahead to ensure all was correct.

It wasn't long before the larger publishing conglomerates erected barricades around their huge spaces. Without appointments no one could break through them, and to solve the problem of those strange folk who might wish to handle the odd book or two at a book fair, huge blow-up photographs of book jackets and their authors adorned the sides of the conglomerate stands. Ironically the only aisles which retained any flavour of what the fair looked like when I first attended it were the remainder outfits. They still stuffed samples of all their ill-gotten wares on trestle tables or wooden boxed cabinets, allowing their customers to handle the goods as the patter was spieled.

Quartet had bought *Tattoo* from Richter at the Frankfurt Fair where Stefan Richter had hustled his way on to our stand and impressed Zelfa Hourani who had asked Stefan to come back later and show his photographs to Naim. Simple, clean and effective – a way of getting published which had been taking place since the Germans invented the book fair at Leipzig in the Middle Ages. Americans invented agents – go figure!

*

I wanted to contribute a short memoir of my working with Naim at Quartet for inclusion in his autobiography. It's still worth a look, I feel...

THE CHAIRMAN PUBLISHES
David Elliott

Fourteen years ago I wrote a book about the book trade, including my years at Quartet. It was an attempt to tell of my experience during what seemed to me was the greatest change to our cultural ethos since the first industrial revolution: the wanton destruction of sustainable work by technology, and the worship of the market.

I do think it lucky I was able to enter the book trade when editorial staff still told their salesmen what was expected of them. I was lucky when Claude Gill Books was bought by a US conglomerate and I saw the last great flowering of the US trade, after the seminal influence of the European émigrés who had fled Nazi Europe transformed American attitudes. I was lucky to run a chain of aggressive metropolitan bookshops able to challenge Net Book Agreement certainty and antiquated retail practices. And, most of all, I was lucky to work at Quartet and the Women's Press.

It was a very special atmosphere. Fourteen years later, I still rejoice that I shared such good times with so diverse an assortment of people, all trying to publish books: radicals and wide boys; captains of industry's daughters; toffs, wastrels and débutantes; feminists and celebrities; earnest and not so earnest writers; intellectuals, wankers and raving loonies. Each day was different, but everything that happened hinged on the attitudes and opinions of the man I called 'the Chairman'.

Anthony Blond, in his memoir *A Jew Made in England*, likened 27 Goodge Street to the Court of Louis XIV. He had a point. Naim once published a brilliant account of life at the Ethiopian Court of Haile Selassie – *The Emperor* by Ryszard Kapuscinski – yet always denied its description of the intrigue and chaos as having any similarity to the dramas and tensions of Goodge Street or the feminist retreat in Shoreditch. Not that the dramas ever interfered with the parties.

I remember being driven terrifyingly fast into a dark German forest by a beautiful princess to drink champagne by a floodlit swimming pool; eating Sunday brunch at Elaine's; being asked to leave the Plaza for wearing inappropriate clothes; watching a man in a gorilla suit doing something rude with a banana in an Amsterdam night club; seeing the sunset over Manama having eaten so many huge lobsters I was ill; my first Broadway show; Covent Garden in the early hours, after a party where champagne and caviar had been consumed by over five hundred guests; telling the Chairman I thought he was nuts not to let Ruby Wax interview Leni Riefenstahl; driving to the Frankfurt Book Fair, and back, in a London taxi cab; escorting Lady Stevens of Ludgate to tea at the Ritz or lunch at the Four Seasons (and she was a Hungarian aristocrat, to boot). And there are, to paraphrase Bennett Cerf's fine publishing memoir, just some memories at random.

Cerf wrote an obituary for Horace Liveright. Now long forgotten, Liveright was a gambler and autocratic publisher whose New York list was one of the most vibrant around in the 1920s. He did change things, founded the Modern Library, but destroyed himself in the process. After a somewhat ambivalent account of Liveright's career, Cerf concludes he: 'had an amazing faculty for winning the unquestioning loyalty of a great number of fine men and women. They love him still. They probably always will… [He had] a rare love of life and a reckless generosity they could not resist.' Like Horace Liveright, the Chairman led a disparate team into many adventures. I remain convinced the real achievement of that unique time was the diversity of talent which was published. Quartet and the Women's Press produced some extraordinary books.

A nd here's just one sample of some of those books, taken once again from *Fulfilment & Betrayal*. It shows just how important a publisher's imprint can be and what has been almost lost by conglomerate greed...

Looking back on 1988, I felt I had been like an actor-manager in that I had spent so much time travelling the country to promote the paperback edition of *Women*. This experience reinforced my conviction that every city, town and village needs well-stocked bookshops. It was disagreeable to see the big bookselling chains jockeying for prime high-street sites in towns that were already adequately served by existing bookshops.

Following on the previous year's success with the Quartet Encounters list [European literature in translation], I decided the time had come to stand the list firmly on its own imprint and issue a separate catalogue with point-of-sale material while orchestrating a major sales campaign in June. Other highlights from the Quartet list at this time were Julia Voznesenskaya's *Letters of Love*, an anthology of messages smuggled out of prisons, asylums and institutions by women prisoners in the Soviet Union; *On the Outside Looking In* which told the harrowing but ultimately uplifting life story of Michael, the adopted son of Ronald Reagan; *Women & Fashion: A New Look* by Caroline Evans and Minna Thornton; and *The Ogre's Embrace* by Rachid Mimouni, translated by Shirley Eber.

The *Nouvel Observateur* had called Mimouni 'the Voltaire of Algiers...one of the great discoveries of French-Algerian literature of recent years'. *Figaro* said he was 'one of the best Algerian contemporary writers...comparable to Kafka and Camus'. The book consisted of seven texts telling of the impact the absurd bureaucracies of the country had on the lives of some of its individual public servants and citizens, from a postal worker to a park keeper to a station master, for instance. There was no escape from those in power for anyone. Mimouni observed it all with a witty eye and a laconic response.

A Marriage Out of Time: My Life with and without Emile Bustani by Laura Bustani, with a preface by John Freeman and a foreword by Mohammed Heikal...told the remarkable story of a Lebanese woman who, after her husband died in an air accident, took over his extensive business interests in the Middle East and guided them through the subsequent years of civil war and invasion. It was also a tribute to the partnership of their marriage before the tragedy. Emile, a Maronite Christian, had been a man of rare integrity, refusing to employ people in his companies on any sectarian basis.

To mark the book's publication there was a party in the ballroom of the Hyde Park Hotel, though, alas, I was not at my best, as the 'Londoner's Diary' in the *Evening Standard* quickly deduced. 'I'm only half the man I usually am,' he announced, propping himself up on a black-and-gold cane. 'I had some surgery on my teeth earlier in the day and I injured my back three days ago. It's not a very manly injury, I'm afraid.'

One of my main objectives in becoming a publisher was to publish books of Middle Eastern interest, covering not only the Palestinian conflict and the suffering of the Palestinian people – which we did comprehensively – but also to promote Arab culture that had been so long ignored in the West. Historically the Arabs of ancient times contributed to the fields of science, medicine, mathematics and the arts. The eclipse of their contribution was largely due to the colonising powers, which for centuries suppressed knowledge of their cultural evolution and almost destroyed the resulting heritage. Tribal strife was another key factor, impeding progress and diverting attention to more mundane pursuits which stifled learning and higher ideals. There remained, however, a rich crop of emerging writers whose work deserved recognition in the West, and especially in the English-speaking world.

I was determined to do my part in having the output translated into English to stand alongside Quartet's international list, which was made up of sometimes obscure or newly discovered talent together with established writers. Although, from the commercial perspective, it was unrealistic to expect good financial returns in the short term, the inclusion of books emanating from or relating to the Middle East enabled Quartet to extend its frontiers to a readership in areas hitherto unknown to it. Leaving politics on one side, our Arab contribution in fiction was substantial. While Zelfa Hourani took charge of the Arab fiction list and developed it to great effect, I remained in direct control of what we published under the headings of non-fiction and politics.

A title of particular importance was Najib Alamuddin's *The Flying Sheikh*, published in 1987, which chronicled the whole story of the founding and establishment of Middle East Airlines, of which he was chairman and president for twenty-five years. Sheikh Najib, who came from an eminent Druze family in Lebanon and became known as 'the Flying Sheikh', had a more detailed understanding than most of the complexities of Lebanese politics. He steered the airline through the stormy passages of Arab-Israeli conflict and sectarian strife in Lebanon, and ultimately ensured its survival in the face of formidable intrigues that had both internal and international origins. In 1993, Quartet went on to publish *Turmoil: The Druzes, Lebanon and the Arab-Israeli Conflict*, in which, with a vivid sense of history, Sheikh Najib traced the origins of the Druzes, of their relationships with other Islamic and Christian groups and of their position in Lebanon's modern times of strife. He had many insights on the influence of the oil wars and the disastrous effects of the international arms trade in the region as a whole.

Dina Abdel Hamid told a more personal story in *Duet for Freedom*, published in 1988, with an introduction by John le

Carré. As a member of the Hashemite dynasty, Princess Dina had been briefly married to King Hussein of Jordan, but her book gave an epic account of events following the capture of her second husband, Salah Ta'amari, a spokesman for the PLO, during the 1982 Israeli invasion of Lebanon. By an extraordinary chance, her attempts to contact Salah and free him from the hidden labyrinth of the notorious prison camp of Ansar, opened up the chance of negotiating with the Israelis for the release of thousands of Palestinians and Lebanese in exchange for six captured Israeli soldiers. *Duet for Freedom* was a true love story with many wider implications. Princess Dina is honorary godmother to our son Ramsay – honorary because of our religious differences, she being of Islamic descent while we belong to the Greek Catholic church.

In 1993 Quartet published Pamela Cooper's lively and readable memoir, *A Cloud of Forgetting*. Pamela's first husband was Patrick Hore-Ruthven, the son of the first Earl of Gowrie, who died on a commando mission in the Western Desert during the Second World War. She was the mother of Grey Gowrie and the Islamic scholar Malise Ruthven and had a long-standing connection with the Middle East from the time when she worked with Freya Stark in Cairo on her Brotherhood of Freedom project, designed to promote ideas of democracy among influential Arabs. With her second husband, Major Derek Cooper, she became active in the post-war years in humanitarian relief work. They were instrumental in founding the charity Medical Aid for Palestinians (MAP) and in 1976 dramatically got themselves expelled from Israel for their outspoken expressions of indignation at the treatment they saw being meted out to Palestinians in the country. For six weeks in 1982 they were trapped in Beirut during the Israeli siege and bombardment in the events leading up to the massacres of Palestinians in Sabra and Chatila. Derek's side of the story of their adventurous life together was told in a biography by John

Baynes, *For Love or Justice: The Life of a Quixotic Soldier*, which Quartet also published three years later.

It was a sign of the mark being made by Quartet that in 1994 Peter Lewis made us the focus of an article in a double-issue of a prestigious literary journal, *Panurge*, entitled 'Quartet & Arab Women'. He selected four Quartet titles: Djura's *The Veil of Silence*, Aïcha Lemsine's *The Chrysalis*, Sabiha Khemir's *Waiting in the Future for the Past to Come* and Hanan al-Shaykh's *Women of Sand and Myrrh*; but first he assessed the situation in British publishing for translations intended for the domestic market.

The situation in general, he concluded, was dire, John Calder's departure in despair for Paris having said much about the 'closed, reactionary intellectual climate in Britain'. Calder and Marion Boyars had previously made great efforts, together and under their separate imprints, to introduce into Britain new writing from abroad, but now silver linings were hard to find. Quartet Books, on the other hand, had 'been pursuing what may be called the Calder-Boyars enterprise with considerable imagination'.

> In 1993, for example, Quartet published fiction and non-fiction titles translated from a number of European languages, including Romanian and Swedish as well as French, Spanish and Russian. In spite of having high reputations in their own countries, most of these authors are unknown in Britain, although the list does include Julien Green, translations of whose fiction first appeared decades ago.
>
> Even more unusual and enterprising, however, has been Quartet's commitment to what it calls the 'Middle East', but which includes most of the Arab world.

The evidence indicated that writing in such countries as Morocco and Algeria was 'flourishing as never before'. The French 'colonial connection and its francophone legacy' meant there was a significantly better situation in France for the publishing of this new literature, but recognition in Britain was still 'barely perceptible'. The common thread in the four books he had under consideration was that their authors' primary purpose was to 'explore and give voice to the experience of women in their cultures', though none of them could be said to be writing feminist polemics. The lack of educational opportunities would have made such attempts at writing impossible for even the preceding generation. Djura, in telling the story of the violence against herself encountered within her own family in *The Veil of Silence* (translated by Dorothy S. Blair), was speaking for all those women 'who keep silent out of fear, who seek a decent life while they are forbidden even to exist'. Yet she still tried to hold on to those positive elements in her heritage that she could identify with, her song troupe, Djurdjura, having the aim of singing 'out loud what their mothers would only murmur under their breath'.

In *The Chrysalis*, Aïcha Lemsine gave a historic sweep to these cultural changes in Algerian society over two generations, where a young woman who has broken free to become a doctor is sucked back into and almost destroyed by the old ways, the situation only being redeemed by her stepmother's defiance of convention and show of womanly solidarity.

Sabiha Khemir's *Waiting in the Future for the Past to Come* was unusual in that it was written in English in the first place. It reached out for a more mythic, storytelling way of giving an account of the changes in women's experiences and expectations in post-independence Tunisia. The collision between tradition and modernity was there, but with 'a sense of new life emerging from the old without a radical severing of connections with the past'.

Hanan al-Shaykh's *Women of Sand and Myrrh* was a follow-up to her first translated novel, *The Story of Zahra*, that Quartet published with success in 1986. *Women of Sand and Myrrh* (translated by Catherine Cobham) interwove the stories of four women living in an unnamed Arab country in the Arabian Gulf. Two of them belong to the country itself, the other two are Lebanese and American respectively. Al-Shaykh, said Lewis, 'is primarily a psychological novelist, exploring the inner lives of her main characters as they try to define themselves through their relationships with women and men...in a social context that inhibits their potential for development and fulfilment'.

In Lewis's view, only one of the four books he had listed would have been available in Britain had there not been a publisher in London committed to issuing 'a substantial number of books in translation'. On the continent most countries – including a large one like Germany with no shortage of writers of its own – had an abundant supply of books translated from English.

> The reverse is not true. To its credit, Quartet has been doing a great deal to rectify this state of affairs, and its advocacy of writers from the Arab world is particularly to be applauded. Very little normally reaches us from these countries, and this is most regrettable when literary activity there is flourishing as never before. Perhaps the next time an Arab writer is awarded the Nobel Prize for Literature, Brits will not look totally mystified and resort to snideries about positive discrimination being exercised in favour of unheard-of second-raters from the Third World.

The following summaries of other selected fiction that we published in this area will help to give the reader a flavour of what was certainly expanding into a major list worthy of close attention. *My Grandmother's Cactus: Stories by Egyptian Women* (translated and introduced by Marilyn Booth) was an anthology of stories by the latest generation of women writers in Egypt. Like some of the others already mentioned, they often featured experiments with new narrative patterns that drew on legend and myth. *Beneath a Sky of Porphyry* (translated by Dorothy S. Blair) was a second novel from Aïcha Lemsine, this one being set at the time of Algeria's war of liberation from the French, telling of the effects of the conflict on the lives of a group of villagers. In much the same vein was *Fantasia: An Algerian Cavalcade* by Assia Djebar (translated by Dorothy S. Blair), which set the life of a young girl against the same background of conflict, based in part on eyewitness accounts of ruthless acts of barbarism by the French colonial forces. *Return to Jerusalem* by Hassan Jamal Husseini, a leading Palestinian diplomat and businessman, was a novel (written in English) that told the story of a Palestinian journalist arrested in Kafkaesque circumstances in Jerusalem by the Israeli security forces and absorbed into Israel's prison system to suffer the authorities' interrogation techniques alternating between brutality and cajolery.

The genre of historical novel was also represented, including an international bestseller, *Leo the African* by Amin Maalouf (translated by Peter Sluglett), based on the colourful life of the sixteenth-century geographer and traveller Leo Africanus, author of the renowned Description of Africa, written in Italy after he had been captured by a Sicilian pirate. *Elissa* by a Tunisian author, Fawzi Mellah (translated by Howard Curtis), was set between the eighth century BC and the present, and concerns a scholar who purports to be translating a letter from a collection of Punic tablets that tells of Elissa's fabulous voyage after fleeing Tyre, which leads to her becoming Queen of Carthage (aka Dido); though he loses track of what he has translated and what he has invented.

Another novel set in Alexandria by Edwar al-Kharrat, *City of Saffron* (translated by Frances Liardet), centred on the growing up of a boy who slowly gains an awareness of the nature of the lives of the adult men and women around him. *Behind Closed Doors: Tales of Tunisian Women* by Monia Hejaiej described the importance of oral storytelling in the lives of three women of Tunis, their views competing and contradictory, in preserving a conservative, moralistic attitude to set against the rebellious and subversive.

From Libya there came a distinguished trilogy, *Gardens of the Night* by Ahmed Faqih (translated by Russell Harris, Amin al-'Ayouti and Suraya 'Allam), published in one volume. It began with *I Shall Present You with Another City*, where the narrator is in Edinburgh as a student, writing a thesis on sex and violence in the Arabian Nights; the second title in the sequence, *These Are the Borders of My Kingdom*, found him back in Libya in a loveless marriage, suffering a breakdown which brings on trances that make him think he is a prince in the Arabian Nights, falling in love with a beautiful princess; and the third was *A Tunnel Lit by One Woman*, in which a female colleague seems to embody the princess of his visions, though the reality gradually evolves towards disillusion.

The theme of North African migrant workers in France was the subject of *Solitaire* by a Moroccan author living in France, Tahar Ben Jelloun. Ben Jelloun had a powerful imagination, as *Solitaire* (translated by Gareth Stanton and Nick Hindley) showed. His twenty-six-year-old central character is condemned by emigration and exile to be trapped in both internal and outward isolation – his own thoughts and the hatred and racism on the streets. Another novel by Ben Jelloun, *The Sand Child*, was the story of a family where the father can produce only daughters, and when the eighth arrives vows that she must be brought up as a boy; with the result that her/his future is marked by the deceptions and hypocrisies that dissect Arab society. The sequel to this, *The Sacred Night* (translated by Alan Sheridan), took up the story of the boy becoming a woman after the father's death, struggling to be reborn in a corrupt, enslaving society through suffering and mutilation. *The Sacred Night* was winner of the 1987 Prix Goncourt.

Quartet meanwhile steadily built up a list of Russian titles reflecting aspects of Soviet and post-Soviet history and Russian culture in general. One of the earliest was Vladimir Kornilov's *Girls to the Front*, the first of this writer's books to appear in English and one which gave an unromanticised portrayal of women conscripted to dig trenches outside Moscow as the Germans advanced on the city in 1941. Novy Mir had accepted it for publication back in 1971 until it was decreed that its description of events in the Great Patriotic War were 'incorrect'. *The Women's Decameron* by Julia Voznesenskaya presented in fictional form the voices of women telling of their experiences under Soviet Communism, using the device of a maternity ward placed under quarantine to bring them together to exchange their stories. Other titles by Voznesenskaya followed. *The Star Chernobyl* (translated by Alan Myers) told a story of three sisters, one of whom, Anna, hears about the disaster at the nuclear plant from abroad and tries to ascertain its extent through her second sister, Anastasia. Both are concerned for the third sister, Aneka, who worked at the power station; Anastasia's search in the 'Dead Zone' leads her into a labyrinth that is a devastating condemnation of official incompetence and deception. *Letters of Love: Women Political Prisoners in Exile and the Camps* was Voznesenskaya's compilation of authentic letters from women prisoners in the Gulag. It prompted Mary Kenny to say in the *Sunday Telegraph* that 'Voznesenskaya could be another Solzhenitsyn'. Edward Kusnetsov's Russian Novel (translated by Jennifer Bradshaw, as was Leonid Borodin's *The Year of Miracle and Grief*) used a 'novel within a novel' technique to illustrate the dangers of non-conformity in an authoritarian conformist society, as one character writes a novel about a friend whose hopes of happiness have been dashed after he has been framed for a crime of which he is innocent. 'The twin faces of Life and Literature grimace from the book like theatre masks,' said the *London Review of Books*. Victor Nekrasov's *Postscripts* (translated by Michael Falchikov and Dennis Ward) was a collection of short stories that welded fact, fiction and memory into elegiac accounts of Russian life from the Great Patriotic War onwards. *Galina Brezhnev and Her Gypsy Lover* by Stanley Laudan was a documentary account of the bizarre relationship between Brezhnev's daughter and the gypsy playboy, thief and con artist Boris Buryata, who used her protection to run spectacular rings round the KGB, till they finally managed to put a stop to his career.

Three relatively little-known novellas by Leo Tolstoy (translated and introduced by Kyril and April Fitzlyon) were published together in one volume: *A Landowner's Morning, Family Happiness and The Devil*. They were all largely autobiographical and written at different points in his career. Fyodor Dostoevsky was represented by *Winter Notes on Summer Impressions* (translated by Kyril Fitzlyon), the first English translation of impressions he gathered from a journey he made to Western Europe – and to Britain – in 1862. There was a major new translation of *The Brothers Karamazov* (by Richard Pevear and Larissa Volokhonsky, who also included annotations), Sidney Monas, of the University of Texas, thinking it: 'Far and away the best translation of Dostoevsky into English that I have seen... Faithful to the original text, and it is, like the original, extremely readable – and a gripping novel.' *Summer in Baden-Baden: From the Life of Dostoevsky* was written as a biographical novel by Leonid Tsypkin (translated by Roger and Angela Keys) and had 'a fantastic realism that burlesques Dostoevsky's own…a crazily marvellous book', thought Victoria Glendinning in the *London Daily News*, while Nikolai Tolstoy said in the Sunday Times that: 'Though a novel, it reproduces real life…persuasively.' Real life was also emphatically there with Dostoevsky's *A Writer's Diary, Volume I: 1873-76* (translated and annotated by Kenneth Lantz and introduced by Gary Saul Morson), which packed over eight hundred pages with an intensive flow of writing that embraced everything from humorous anecdotes to trial reports, autobiography, philosophy, polemics and original stories. Besides writing it, the author had made the time to edit and issue it as a monthly publication.

In parallel with these other developments, the Quartet Encounters list, presided over by Stephen Pickles, continued to grow prodigiously. It kept to its literary focus in the main, though widened its scope to bring in other items of international cultural interest. Lou Andreas-Salomé's *The Freud Journal* (translated by Stanley W. Leavy and introduced by Mary-Kay Wilmers) was a personal view of Freud's studies and relations with colleagues against the background of a literary coterie that included the poet Rilke; Rilke himself was represented by *Rodin and Other Prose Pieces*, he having at one time been secretary to the great sculptor (translated by G. Craig Huston and introduced by William Tucker), *Early Prose*, which included memories as well short fiction pieces, and his *Selected Letters 1902-1926* (translated by R. F. C. Hull and introduced by John Bayley). Gaston Bachelard's *The Psychoanalysis of Fire* (translated by Alan M. C. Ross and introduced by Northrop Frye) was an idiosyncratic exploration of ideas concerning fire in human evolution and their symbolic and subconscious connotations.

Bruno Walter's *Gustav Mahler* (translated by Lotte Walter Lindt and introduced by Michael Tanner) was an indispensable source book for any study of the composer, coming from the foremost interpreter of his music, who had been deeply and personally involved in realising much of it in performance.

With over a score of other titles to choose from, the following list can only be highly selective, but will show the consistency of quality achieved by Pickles.

Hermann Broch, the son of a Jewish textile manufacturer in Vienna, was an industrialist, mathematician and philosopher who came to literature reluctantly as the only way of expressing his thoughts and feelings. *The Guiltless* (translated by Ralph Manheim with an afterword by the author) was a book he called 'a novel in eleven stories'; it portrayed a group of eleven lives in the pre-Hitler period. *The Sleepwalkers*, one of his major achievements (translated by Willa and Edwin Muir and introduced by Michael Tanner), was a trilogy that traced from the 1880s the social erosion and dissolution that culminated in the Nazi era. Another Viennese novelist of stature was Heimito von Doderer, who was an active Nazi up to 1938. His vast trilogy, *The Demons* (translated by Willa and Edwin Muir and introduced by Michael Hamburger), explored every strand of life possible in Vienna, both comic and tragic, where the 'demons' concerned arose from people's minds in the tumultuous years between the two world wars. Thomas Bernhard was born in Holland but grew up in Austria and wrote in German, becoming, George Steiner considered, 'one of the masters of contemporary European fiction' in the post-war years. *Concrete* (translated by Martin McLintock and introduced by Martin Chalmers) was a story in his 'black idyll' style about a writer who goes away to start a project but

160

finds himself obsessively following an altogether different line of inquiry set off by a tragic memory. *On the Mountain* (translated by Russell Stockman with an afterword by Sophie Wilkins) showed him working in parallel with themes to be found in Kafka and Beckett in a novel written as one sentence.

E. M. Cioran had been born in Romania in 1911, but had won a scholarship in Paris and subsequently made the decision to live in France and write in French, though he said he had no nationality – 'the best possible status for an intellectual'. He was regarded as a foremost contemporary European thinker, the heir of Kierkegaard, Nietzsche and Wittgenstein, who wrote incomparable, elegantly styled essays on the state of man in the modern world. Five of his collections found a place on the list (four of them being translated by Richard Howard): *Anathemas and Admirations* (introduced by Tom McGonigle), in which incisive estimates of literary figures were interspersed with caustic aphorisms; *A Short History of Decay* (introduced by Michael Tanner), whose theme was the 'philosophical viruses' of the twentieth century; *The Temptation to Exist* (introduced by Susan Sontag), a 'dance of ideas and debates' on 'impossible states of being'; and *The Trouble with Being Born* (introduced by Benjamin Ivry), which started out with the proposition that the disaster of life begins with the fact of birth, 'that laughable accident'. The fifth title (translated and introduced by Ilinca Zarifopol-Johnston) was *On the Heights of Despair*, a youthful work, written in Romania, which showed him to be already a 'theoretician of despair'.

Representing Swedish literature was, first, Stig Dagerman, whom Michael Meyer thought to be 'the best writer of his generation in Sweden and one of the best in Europe'. *A Burnt Child* (translated by Alan Blair and introduced by Laurie Thompson) was set in Stockholm in a family where the mother has died, the drama being played out between the husband and son and, respectively, the father's ageing mistress and the son's timid fiancée. *German Autumn* (translated and introduced by Robin Fulton) gave a documentary portrait of the Germans in defeat immediately after the fall of the Third Reich which courageously saw them as suffering individuals. *The Games of Night* (translated by Naomi Walford and introduced by Michael Meyer) was a collection of stories showing his versatility. *The Snake* (translated by Laurie Thompson) was a tour de force where the threads of disparate stories, arising from a conscript army camp, are brought together in a denouement. Then came Sweden's Nobel Prize-winning Pär Lagerkvist who had two titles in the list: *The Dwarf* (translated by Alexandra Dick and introduced by Quentin Crewe), a dark historical tale of a Machiavellian dwarf at the Court of a Renaissance prince; and *Guest of Reality* (translated and introduced by Robin Fulton), a set of three stories linking the growing of a boy into a young man. A major novel of social concern from Sweden was Per Olov Enquist's *The March of the Musicians* (translated by Joan Tate), which told about the political uprising of the workers in a remote northern part of the country against their exploitation by sawmill owners and browbeating by hellfire preachers on Sundays; the author's profound empathy with his characters gave this small episode in Sweden's labour history a universal resonance.

Gabriele D'Annunzio was a leading writer of the so-called Decadent school. *The Flame* (translated and introduced by Susan Bassnett) was his scandalous novel about a passionate affair between a young writer and a great actress, in which they battle for supremacy in love and art; it was scandalous because based on his own relationship with Eleanora Duse. *Nocturne and Five Tales of Love and Death* (translated and introduced by Raymond Rosenthal) was a selection of his prose fiction demonstrating what a formidable pioneer

D'Annunzio had been as a writer. Equally pioneering was his compatriot and contemporary Luigi Pirandello, known mainly for his experimental plays, though his short stories were also among the greatest in literature. Those selected for *Short Stories* (translated and introduced by Frederick May) showed his concern with the masks people use socially and their interplay with the reality behind them. Elio Vittorini was a writer from Sicily who aimed for 'neo-realism' in his work and produced an undisputed masterpiece in *Conversations in Sicily* (translated by Wilfrid David and introduced by Stephen Spender): first published in 1939, the censorship it was constrained by gave it an underlying power in the story of a young man's journey back to Sicily to console his mother after his father had deserted her.

From the next generation, Pier Paolo Pasolini was seen primarily as a film-maker of originality in Britain, though in his native Italy he was regarded rather more as a poet, critic and novelist. Helping to rectify our view were *A Dream of Something* (translated and introduced by Stuart Hood), a story about three friends from northern Italy whose search for money takes them abroad, though they return home to political violence and an end to their carefree roistering; *Theorem* (translated and introduced by Stuart Hood), which was written in tandem with the making of a film of the same title, in which Terence Stamp played the young man gaining a sexual, emotional and intellectual hold over a rich bourgeois family; and *Roman Nights and Other Stories* (translated by John Shepley and introduced by Jonathan Keates), a selection of five stories from Pasolini's miscellaneous writings that reflected the cultural changes taking place in post-war Italian society.

Yevgeny Zamyatin chose exile from Soviet Russia in 1931, foreseeing the clash between writers and the state that lay ahead. *A Soviet Heretic* (translated by Mirra Ginsburg and introduced by Alex M. Shane) was a collection of his writings on fellow writers and the condition of literature in the Soviet Union, as well as his letter to Stalin, seeking voluntary exile, and his letter of resignation from the Soviet Writers' Union. The status of Osip Mandelstam as the pre-eminent Russian poet of the twentieth century gave him no protection from murderous NKVD brutality. *The Noise of Time and Other Prose Pieces* (collected, translated and introduced by Clarence Brown) was a selection from the range of his writing, including a work of invective and outrage against the state's official campaign against him. Yury Tynyanov's *Lieutenant Kijé & Young Vitushishnikov* (translated and introduced by Mirra Ginsburg) were two glittering novellas by a Russian master satirist about abuses in the eighteenth and nineteenth centuries which allowed him to be obliquely critical of those of the Soviet regime. Abram Tertz, the nom de plume for Andrei Synyavsky in his samisdat publications (that won him hard labour and exile), wrote *Little Jinx* (translated by Larry P. Joseph and Rachel May and introduced by Edward J. Brown) as a black farce containing the line: 'Were we not guilty, neither Hitler nor Stalin could have surfaced among us.' *The Fatal Eggs & Other Soviet Satire* (translated, edited and introduced by Mirra Ginsburg) was a famous subversive anthology by seventeen boldly comic writers, including Mikhail Bulgakov, Ilf and Petrov and Zamyatin.

There were also the stories of Aharon Appelfeld, with their subtle and profound recreations of life in Europe's Jewish communities as they moved into the gathering shadows of the Holocaust; and Giorgio Bassani's artistic account of the impact on a Jewish family in Italy as Mussolini's fascism geared up the anti-Semitic component in its laws under pressure from Nazi Germany. Those titles have been given earlier, with the list of Jewish authors published by Quartet. Another important aspect of the Quartet Encounters list was the way it demonstrated the importance of literature in delineating the dimensions of human experience and suffering within the history of the twentieth century's traumatic events. While this summary of the list has not by any means been comprehensive, it is enough to show there was a spirit of adventure at work in Goodge Street for which it would have been hard to find an equivalent elsewhere in British publishing at the time.

> *Mr Rosenthal, who retired from Harvard Press in 1990, was seventy when he started his last job, as publisher of Hill & Wang, a division of Farrar, Straus & Giroux. In an interview at the time, Mr Rosenthal acknowledged that the business was becoming more difficult. But his enthusiasm was a constant. 'Something happens,' he said. 'You get an idea. You meet an author. You can't be depressed and be a good publisher.'*
> **Publishers Weekly**

> *As a boy I saw authors for a number of years from the other side of the publisher's counter, at an angle from which they seemed small and often tiresome. I cannot rid myself of this early vision. Only the great ones have magnanimity; the rest, whatever their 'carapace', are self-distrustful and morbidly sensitive creatures who, if their work does not sell, cherish a gnawing grievance, and if it does sell, are subjected to the contempt of those whom they regard as the envious few.*
> **Frank Swinnerton, *Figures in the Foreground* (1964)**

It was another country fifty years ago, but did we do things so differently? Let's get back to the 'gaffer' – Basil Blackwell and his right book in the right place for the right price at the right time. It was every bookseller's ambition after all to manage an efficient customer order department. It was said that Elsie Bertram would not let her staff leave the henhouse where the books were dispatched until every order received that morning had been either dispatched or reported on. Stanley Unwin refused to increase his overall discount to bookshops pointing out the cost of maintaining a staff and organisation capable of supplying any Allen & Unwin title in print by return. Book Centre, a vast barren space on the North Circular Road which ran a shared warehouse with over ninety publishers of all sizes and intention, could sometimes take six weeks to fulfil supply, especially when they boasted of implementing a new computer system which was to transform their capabilities. Not that they were alone. This was the time that experts in logistics and critical path analysis had begun to appear.

The now almost forgotten Robert Maxwell, who with a bit more luck and a better sense of timing might have destroyed Rupert Murdoch's burgeoning English publishing empire before his own was done for, boasted of becoming the first British publisher to purchase a large computer called a 'main-frame'. A coachload of important booksellers were driven to Headington Hill Hall, where Maxwell maintained his Pergamon Press warehouse, to stand on a hillside as Maxwell's helicopter landed and the enormous man bellowed that we follow him into a large air-conditioned office block to face a number of huge green constructs with flashing lights, attended by staff in white coats and face masks. We were required to don similar garb in the vestibule before we entered the cavernous room with a slightly sinister whirling humming noise. We passed through two glass doors to face some large green steel monoliths with blinking lights and what appeared to be spinning tapes of a brown plastic-like substance which seemed to account for the whirling noise.

The white-coated, masked attendants silently moved from monolith to monolith lifting the odd flap or pressing the odd button. We were passed along the room until, at the last monolith, a stream of paper was appearing which was being bound into a huge roll. Maxwell was a charmer when it suited him and with his nicest smile, he boomed out the message that Pergamon Press had become the first English publisher to fully ('fully' was said very boomily – Maxwell never quite lost his mid-European twang) – integrate ('integrate' had a guttural, rolling 'r') their entire invoice and order processing division.

The group of booksellers looked as impressed as they could manage and then were whisked away to a picnic buffet in the grounds. We had seen the future. Soon most publishers with large inventory, in ever larger warehouses 'fully integrated', closing for weeks at a time and usually running late deliveries for some weeks after the announced date for all to be up and running. The London trade counters, where we could pick up, often on the same day as the customer ordered a copy, were closed. Order vouchers backed up with delivery notes, written in biro pen, or carbon copies of such, as the originals were needed to send an invoice in the post the next day, became obsolete.

And actual people disappeared. The man at the Heinemann London Trade Counter, just up from the Curzon cinema in Mayfair, could tell you the exact position of hundreds of Heinemann books, whether reprinting, out of print or not yet published. He was quicker than Google, more effective than the Amazon computer, and he disappeared. As did most of the Grub Street we knew…

In a town like London there are always plenty of not-quite-certifiable lunatics walking the streets, and they tend to gravitate towards bookshops, because a bookshop is one of the few places where you can hang about for a long time without spending any money.

George Orwell

'The chief evil of the bookselling trade,' wrote Michael Joseph in 1949 in *The Adventure of Publishing*, 'is something which has for many years been proclaimed a virtue. "Come in and browse... You will not be pressed to buy."' I quoted it in a chapter of *A Trade of Charms*, published in 1992. 'One man's account of over twenty-five years spent in the British book trade,' said my jacket blurb. 'He has seen a sleepy, comfortable trade try to become and aggressive modern business... It is the author's opinion that we are witnessing the destruction of all that was once good about a trade he loved... Bad, silly men have ravaged, with their buying, selling and merging – and for greed – the book trade that I joined. They have created "a business" where there seems no difference between the way books are sold from the way of any other commodity. They have changed the trade that I came to love, for no good reason save that they thought books were the same as shoes. They are wrong...'

I tried to describe how I'd been taught to peddle books like dope: understand the addict's tastes and feed the habit. I wasn't aware of Laetitia Hawkins's account of London bookshops in 1835, as I had yet to discover Rosemary Gray's delectable anthology of Literary London, published by the Collector's Library, where I discovered this account:

> The shop of Payne, the bookseller, at the Mews Gate, was at this time the resort of the London literati. This place was as little calculated as any could well be for the reception of the number who not only frequented

it but at certain hours of the day were never out of it. It was, as is well known, though probably the traces of it may soon be gone, at the gate of the lower Mews, opening into Castle Street, Leicester Fields; an elbow-shed rather than shop and lighted by a skylight. Crossing obliquely the gate of the Mews, Payne had a good dwelling house the ground-floor windows of which were fairly barricaded with books.

In this nookery were to be found, about one every day, such men as the Revd Mr Cracherode, Mr Southwell, Mr Tyrrwhitt, the Bishop of Dromore (Dr Percy), Dr Heberden, Bennet Langton, George Stevens, Sir J. Hawkins, and others. Mr Cracherode, Mr Tyrrwhitt and Mr Southwell were as regular as the day itself, much to the annoyance of Payne, who found them very much in the way; the rest were occasionally, but very generally, to be seen there.

With a hope of attracting some of these literary loungers, Henry Payne, a younger brother of Johnson's publisher, opened a very handsome shop, almost opposite Marlborough House, in Pall Mall, but the business was not brisk. The owner used to remark on the vexatious power of habit, which made these gentlemen, so desirable visitors to him, prefer his namesake's dark, dirty, encumbered shop to his, which was certainly in all points very attractive.

Laetitia's notebooks were published in 1836, a year after her death. She would become a character in Beryl Bainbridge's novel *According to Queeney*, but she's forgotten everywhere else. Her father was Samuel Johnson's friend, hence the name-dropping reference above, and she mixed with 'literary loungers' most of her life. It may well be that networking events in Hoxton, or literary book club evenings in a local Waterstones (Laetitia lived in Twickenham, with her brother and her lady companion – according to Richard Cobbett, the threesome 'formed as grotesque a trio as can well be imagined'), are just as lively as those were at Payne, the booksellers, but somehow I think not.

> *A writer can go far if he combines a certain talent for dramatisation and a facility for speaking everyone's language, with the art of exploiting the passions, the concerns of the moment.*
>
> **Gustave Flaubert**

But a bookseller, even perhaps a publisher, needs what Boswell discovered about his mentor: 'Dr Johnson had a peculiar facility in seizing at once what was valuable in any book without submitting to the labour of perusing it from beginning to end.' I imagine those dope peddlers who at last might suck the odd teat of merchandise from time to time, but constant use would render the merchant incapable of maintaining a truly commercial enterprise.

Do betting shop owners bet? Or publicans become alcoholics? I always suspected potential staff at bookshop interviews who announced their 'love of reading' highly suspicious and almost certainly useless. You can discover this characteristic easily enough these days perusing the Waterstones' staff picks sections. Few have heeded Somerset Maugham's advice: 'The wise reader will get the greatest enjoyment out of reading literature if he learns the useful art of skipping...but to skip without loss is not easy.'

Or else, the ultimate horror: attend a literary festival! In recent years the literary festival has become huge business. For some reason the abuse heaped on Amazon's doorstep for its supposedly aggressive demand for discounts (no more often than that demanded by Waterstones) or its insistence that it pays its taxes according to the tax laws set by elected parliaments, rather than 'morality', is never aimed at the ever burgeoning world of literary-festivising. Let's just see what's involved from a publisher's point of view (and don't forget that most of these events are set up as literary 'charities', and that's not even listing the number of events supported by our cash via the funding from the Arts Council or local authorities – or usually, both).

The publisher normally funds their writers' expenses – travel, hospitality, even room and board if the author has to be there overnight. There is often a charge for a mention in the programme, a request to contribute towards the wine and cheese and, the final insult, a demand for excessively high discounts and the right to return any unsold copies irrespective of the condition after dumping boxes on soggy grass in leaking marquees. To rub in the salt, the organisers charge an outright entrance fee to Joe Public to see and hear the author, which they simply pocket outright.

In a recent BBC 4 Radio programme describing the career of Nora Smallwood, her successor at the helm of Chatto & Windus, Carmen Callil sniffed that Nora told her no Chatto author ever spoke to the press. The publishing wonder woman was appalled. No wonder Ms Smallwood was past her sell-by date. Publicity was all. Ed Victor, the greatest literary agent in the history of literary agents, until Andrew Wylie helped Martin Amis get new teeth, called publicity 'an oxygen'. Nora Smallwood went the way of her imprint, as did most of the other charismatic publishers who walked along our Grub Street. All the great imprints were merged, suppressed or buried into vast multinational hybrids. Imprints became marketing labels and if Amazon win the ebook battle, even more will cease to mean anything to the literary festival goer. Us old grubbers regarded an imprint as a guide above all else to a publisher's taste, for taste was what we were about.

The English language is like a broad river on whose bank a few patient anglers are sitting, while, higher up, the stream is being pouted by a string of refuse-barges tipping out their muck.

Cyril Connolly

Really the writer doesn't want success. He knows that he has a short span of life, that the day will come when he must pass through the wall of oblivion, and he wants to leave a scratch on the wall – Kilroy was here – that somebody a hundred, or a thousand years later will see.

William Faulkner

I still remember the contempt a thrusting young manager of the Waterstones at Camden Town, who wrote a column for the equally defunct *Publishing News*, when he mentioned my book of memoirs. He, and all his ilk, rejected my whimsical, fuddy-duddy ways. Modern retail bookselling was about logistical control of minimum stock levels, 'rolled out' in brightly-lit shop units with space and sofas. Inventory was managed by computers at special points where customer queries were answered so long as the customer knew the proper title or how the author's name was spelt. Waterstones went bust two times, though its founder didn't do that badly out of it. Each time, the publishers took a hit, clearing historical debts or crediting millions of pounds of returned stock, often completely unsaleable. All this coincided with the write-offs of millions of pounds as British publishers merged and conglomerated even further into outposts of firstly American, and then as the Americans were bought and sold, European media conglomerates. In the space of less than ten years no general publisher of any consequence was still owned by their original founders, or any home-grown, independent British publisher remaining native-owned.

And Waterstones had been yet again rescued, this time by a Russian oligarch, merging with the independent London-based posh people's travel bookshops, Daunt Books.

As the Thatcher government used the income from North Sea oil to pay the measly social security for the millions of workers her policies threw out of work, so writers and woefully underpaid booksellers bore the brunt of Grub Street's disintegration. For Grub Street had always been a mirror-image for the times it saw. If you want to really know what it was like in medieval London, read Chaucer; Georgian Bath, Jane Austen and life between the wars, *Hanover Square*. But it also mirrored what was to happen in other service industries, as we were taught to call them.

I worked with spivs from time to time. Grub Street attracted them. Some even made significant changes, but spivs were never centre-stage and hardly ever invited to top tables. The conglomerates changed all that, but by then the spivs were everywhere – in government, banking, education. Children no longer wanted to be explorers or parsons. They wanted Richard Branson to run the country and watched Alan Sugar fire people. Television game shows garner more votes when viewers must decide who won than do local government elections. Hundreds of thousands of supposedly grown-up people queued up, some for days, outside bookshops dressed as Dumbledore or Harry Potter when the final volume in his series of adventures was published at a minute past midnight, all around the world.

Her finely touched spirit had still its fine issues, though they were not widely visible. Her full nature, like that river of which Cyrus broke the strength, spent itself in channels which had no great name on the earth. But the effect of her being on those around her was incalculably diffusive: for the growing good of the world is partly dependent on unhistoric acts; and that things are not so ill with you and me as they might have been, is half owing to the number who lived faithfully a hidden life, and rest in unvisited tombs.

George Eliot, *Middlemarch*

I can't complain. Those of us who walked down Grub Street in its glory days had some glorious times. Hopefully some of the anecdotes in the past pages show this; if not, apologies, for they were meant to. I saw places, met people, did things I never thought would be possible for someone from my class and background. The book trade gave me a privileged life. I don't share the fury that Amazon will destroy it all, even if it does. It's the privileged life that I see the young folk missing and that's far more serious than the moral outrage from people whose vested interests have been bashed about by Amazon's remorseless indifference to anything other than its customers' needs.

Amazon still hasn't made a profit. It seems as illusory as was Tim Waterstone's worldwide empire of huge bookshops was to become. But for the time being no one cares. It's turning over too much money. And, like the banks, it will become too big to allow its collapse, if collapse it does. Waterstones were saved by the book trade incorporating its losses in order to ensure its branches stayed open – a mirror image of the Royal Bank of Scotland.

The book trade will be destroyed, as most decent things are, by being hi-jacked by people who have no sense of why we got to where we did and how we managed to do it in the first place. Our past predicts our future. The man who sat in the trade counter at William Heinemann ensuring all the London bookshops could have their orders the next day wasn't paid that much, I'd hazard. He certainly complained about how Thomas Tilling – then the owners of the publishers – wasted money on away-day training sessions which taught him leadership skills. I sometimes wondered if he ever actually read a book, but he knew his lists inside out. He also loved the trade. He even remembered when Graham Greene used the staff flat, perched above the trade counter, and suggested slightly improper reasons for the great writer staying there. Gossip was a huge source of Grub Street energy.

I mention him and preface it with George Eliot's epic final sentence to pay him homage. In this age of constant texting and tableting, fiddling and faddling on tiny machines with widgits in our ears, it may well be that books will cease to delight. Fewer will be made and most post-Grub-Street energies will be spent on selling huge amounts of fewer titles. Diversity and difference will be trumped by correctness and conformity.

But whatever route the new Grub Street takes in this digital world, if we lose the curmudgeon who remembered the 'good old times' or the ancient irritating gnome who says that's not how things were done, the book trade will lose its soul.

Literary men are a perpetual priesthood.
Thomas Carlyle

Publishing is still a cheap enough way to garner attention. With a bit of luck and, if the product is well enough made, the book will outlive all that the multi-million pound entertainment conglomerates try as they 'rationalise' its production. For some crazies will always want to write, the poets to pronounce, the wild gypsies in the woods to still search for publication, in the belief and hope that someone, somewhere still remembers Grub Street and what we stood for and wants to join the club.

> *Literary men are the children of their age, and so like all the rest of the lot must subordinate themselves to external conditions of living together. They must be absolutely decent.*
>
> **Anton Chekhov**

Anthony Blond once declared that the way to make a small fortune in publishing was to start out with a large one. Much shrewder than he always insisted that he wasn't, his Grub Street credentials were top dog. Louche, often drunken and always leery, his acid tongue could be as quick as his darting eyes. He worked the room, charmingly relentless in his pursuit of wherever his next pleasure might be found. He joined Quartet as consulting editor with his own imprint – 'An Anthony Blond Book' – just as his reputation began to wane, though that reputation still had some stardust.

He'd started with Allan Wingate before setting up on his own in 1958. His earliest books included Simon Raven's *The Feathers of Death* (1959), the first of a long succession of Raven novels for Blond, many of which might never have been written had not Blond insisted Raven move out of London and take a monthly wage, payable only as the wayward Raven completed his brilliantly funny *Alms for Oblivion* series and *A History of Orgies* (1958) by Burgo Partridge, son of Ralph and Frances Partridge, sold in the United States, an unbelievable feat at the time for an unknown English imprint, and an early indication of Blond's eternal interest in kinky sex.*

---

* Simon Raven is shamefully ignored, a victim to the relentless feminisation of popular literary culture. He was spectacularly Grub Street. His wife sent him a telegram once: 'Wife and baby starving send money soonest' to receive the reply: 'Sorry no money suggest eat baby.'

He published Spike Milligan's first novel, *Puckoon*, in 1963; other bestsellers included Harold Robbins's *The Carpetbaggers* and William Peter Blatty's *The Exorcist*. He commissioned E. F. Schumacher's *Small is Beautiful* (1973), always claiming the title was his invention. In due course Desmond Briggs, who had worked for the firm for some time, became a partner and the firm became Blond & Briggs, but partnerships were not Blond's forte and acrimony was never far away. Briggs left and a brief merger with another small independent list became Muller, Blond & White but in 1987 Blond's publishing career came to an end as the conglomerate then called Hutchinson swallowed up the Muller, Blond & White list. And that was how he came to Quartet.

In his autobiography, *Jew Made in England* (commissioned by a fearless toff publisher, Gerard Noel, who bravely lost a small fortune running Timewell Press, Blond's last publisher), he printed his own obituary as the book's foreword. Of his coming to Quartet he wrote:

> Although an energetic spotter of talent, Blond lacked the discipline and temperance to make a good businessman, and was, according to his friends, trusting and gullible. He was now bereft, having regarded an imprint as a form of self-expression.
>
> Blond attempted to secure work through his extensive network in what he liked to call the 'publishing game'. No one wanted to know: and Blond was quoted as saying, 'None of my best friends are Jews.' Nevertheless, he was taken up out of charity, by the Palestinian Arab Naim Attallah, as a consultant to his firm, Quartet.

Retiring to his house in France pretty soon after his 'consultancy', now to be carried out by fax and rather badly connected telephone calls, he asked if he could attend the

Frankfurt Book Fair to celebrate his new relationship. A request Naim agreed to even after Anthony managed to chip an ankle bone on a French cobblestone, requiring him to sit in a wheelchair with his right leg in plaster, and a foot sticking out with toes showing for all to see. His major preoccupation during the fair, apart from having numerous foreign publishers sign his plaster cast and sing every night he attended, alongside Stephen Pickles, Quartet's editorial director at the time, medieval plainsong – both liked the echo of their voices in the car-park basement at Naim's Wiesbaden hotel – was to attempt to convince Naim, a strident heterosexual, that careful manipulation of a finger in a gentleman's arsehole could arouse ecstasies unknown in male/female trysts.

My other memory was his habit of stuffing the bread rolls, ham, cheese and sliced tomatoes, made available in our hotel's breakfast buffet, into a plastic shower cap, also provided for free in his en suite bedroom. When I remonstrated with him, his contempt was withering. Proper publishers are constantly looking to cut costs. The breakfast was included in the hotel rate and lunch prices in the fairgrounds were extortionate. (Some years later when I went to the international children's book fair at Bologna, I was intrigued to see a fair number of English lady publishers sitting in the Italian sunshine, all removing rolls, cheese and ham from their hotel room shower caps.)

Anthony Blond sparkled in a time when proprietorial outrageousness was still tolerated. A publisher could misbehave in order to defend his list. He never had the power or range of say Allen Lane who could still organise the destruction of over six thousand paperbacks as he disliked the book cover design brought in by the new management in his recently reconstructed beloved Penguin Books. But Blond had had bestsellers and helped show the conglomerates the future – brash covers, gossip column coverage, wild parties to launch new titles. Yet he also understood the Hollywood writers' hairy old axiom: 'Shit has its own integrity.' It let him down. Carmen Callil once said something intelligent about publishing. You only ever understand the zeitgeist for about ten years and then you lose the plot. Blond did, but he always kept that other publishing skill: luck.

And perhaps this book has traces of lost plots. Maybe the Grub Street we think isn't there any more is really just around a corner we've missed. It is actually alive and well in Hoxton but nobody wants whingeing old creeps at their party.

We hope so.